Correction Notice

Andrea Pin, *Religious Freedom without the Rule of Law*. ISBN 978-90-04-53323-3 (paperback); ISBN 978-90-04-53322-6 (e-book). Leiden, The Netherlands: Brill | Nijhoff. https://doi.org/10.1163/9789004533226. The book, published in the series Brill's Research Perspectives in Law and Religion, was published online on 16 September 2024 and in print on 26 September 2024.

The author has brought to Brill's attention, based on feedback from readers, that the following phrase on p. 26, set in italics, is incorrect: "Chaldean Catholics—who number less than one million—belong to *the Assyrian ethnic group*, one of the first populations to embrace Christianity."

The italicized phrase has been deleted (and 'less' replaced by 'fewer') so that the text now reads: "Chaldean Catholics—who number fewer than one million—belong to one of the first populations to embrace Christianity."

De Gruyter Brill, 27 November 2024

 | DOI:10.1163/9789004533226_CORR

Religious Freedom without the Rule of Law

Law and Religion

Volumes published in this Brill Research Perspectives title are listed at *brill.com/rplrs*

Religious Freedom without the Rule of Law

The Constitutional Odysseys of Afghanistan, Egypt, and Iraq and the Fate of the Middle East

By

Andrea Pin

BRILL | NIJHOFF

LEIDEN | BOSTON

Library of Congress Control Number: 2024944084

Typeface for the Latin, Greek, and Cyrillic scripts: "Brill". See and download: brill.com/brill-typeface.

ISSN 2468-2985
ISBN 978-90-04-53323-3 (paperback)
ISBN 978-90-04-53322-6 (e-book)
DOI 10.1163/9789004533226

This book is printed on acid-free paper and produced in a sustainable manner.

Contents

Acknowledgments

I am deeply grateful to Norman Doe and John Witte, Jr., for welcoming this work within the Brill Research Perspectives in Law and Religion series that they co-lead. This book stems from years of research and conversations with experts in law and international relations, without whom it would have never seen the light of day.

A lot of inspiration came from years of intense collaboration with the Oasis Foundation in Venice and Milan. Several debates and informal chats with Vittorio Emanuele Parsi and Riccardo Redaelli were crucial to understanding the Middle East and why fundamental categories of the rule of law fail to apply in the region. I feel privileged to have been included among the McDonald Distinguished Senior Fellows of 2024–2029 of the Center for the Study of Law and Religion at Emory University. I lost track of how many times have I had to thank John Witte, Jr. (John has failed me only when he took me and my son fishing) and the Center for the Study of Law and Religion at large, which has been so helpful throughout the writing process. The help of Whittney Barth and Amy Wheeler has been critical, as have been the editorial input of Ellen Wert and the comments of two anonymous reviewers.

Heartfelt thanks go to Tommaso Edoardo Frosini for encouraging me to take a fresh look at the logic of the rule of law in a book that I published within his series[1] and to the Notre Dame Religious Freedom Initiative, which invited me to present on religious freedom in the Middle East.[2] I am deeply grateful to Francesco Biagi, who was so kind to read the manuscript and offer very useful comments.

If there is one thing that I learned from the Middle East, that is that there is no such thing as *the Middle East*. There are several *Middle Easts* living—and often struggling—together. It is a type of extreme pluralism—much more extreme than the one Westerners like me are used to. If this small work helps to make it slightly more understandable to the rest of the world, it will have done its job. By showing the distance between the Middle Eastern and the Western models of constitutionalism, I want to bring the two of them a little closer so they can better understand each other.

---

1 Andrea Pin, *Il* rule of law *come problema: le sfide dell'Europa centro-orientale, della Brexit e del Medio Oriente* (Naples: Edizioni scientifiche, 2021).

2 Andrea Pin, "Religious Persecution and Constitution Building in the Middle East: The Rule-of-Law Conundrum," *Notre Dame Law Review Reflection* 97, no. 3 (2022): 245–63. This book draws in part on this source.

I dedicate this book to the people of the Middle East who are so dear to my heart. I conceived of the volume when ISIS was at its sunset in Syria and Iraq, and I finish it while Israel is sieging Gaza, where hostages are held, and Lebanon is in turmoil. I wish my book were not so timely.

Religious Freedom without the Rule of Law

The Constitutional Odysseys of Afghanistan, Egypt, and Iraq and the Fate of the Middle East

Andrea Pin
Department of Public, International and Community Law,
University of Padua, Italy
andrea.pin@unipd.it

Abstract

Religious Freedom without the Rule of Law: The Constitutional Odysseys of Afghanistan, Egypt, and Iraq and the Fate of the Middle East compares the domestic and international efforts to instill the values and practices of the rule of law in the Middle East in the early twenty-first century with their disappointing performances in terms of safety, political volatility, human rights violations, and, especially, religious freedom. It zooms in on Afghanistan, Egypt, and Iraq to argue that international interventions and local struggles underestimated the ethno-religious mosaic of these countries and their ideological cleavages. The rule of law could not reasonably replace local rights and promote religious freedom as many hoped. The notions of individualism, equality, rights, and courts, which are among the strongest philosophical underpinnings of the rule of law, are explored and contrasted with the political and constitutional culture of the Middle East. The work concludes that securing stability and protecting religious freedom in the region requires compromising on the rule of law and that the consociational model of constitutionalism would probably have better chances of achieving them.

Keywords

Middle East – rule of law – religious freedom – Afghanistan – Egypt – Iraq – Islamic law – individualism – rights – courts – consociations

Introduction

The year 2024 marks the twentieth anniversary of the 2004 constitution of Afghanistan, which entered into force after an international alliance under the

 | DOI:10.1163/9789004533226_002

UN umbrella toppled the Taliban regime.[1] In August 2021, after seventeen years spent trying to enforce the constitution and its new order, the United States left in a hurry only to be replaced by the Taliban in a major comeback. After establishing the Islamic Emirate of Afghanistan,[2] the Taliban are struggling to control the territory, as they are resisted by parts of the civil society that do not want to be governed by them and by the local branch of the Islamic State (ISIS).

The year 2024 marks also the tenth anniversary of the 2014 constitution of Egypt, now in force. After a few years of hope, turmoil, and violence, the 2014 constitution encapsulated the resurrection of the forces that backed the decades-long leader Hosni Mubarak. The hopes of the 2010 Arab Spring soon materialized in Egypt with the end of Mubarak's rule and the replacement of the 1971 constitution with a transitional constitutional declaration (2011). The Muslim Brotherhood seized power in 2012 and elected Mohammad al-Morsi, a member of their party, as president of the republic. Morsi oversaw the 2012 constitution-making process, which was supposed to symbolize the end of Mubarak's regime. However, Morsi's constitution lasted less than one year; Morsi himself was soon forced to leave and was incarcerated; he later died in jail (2019). Mohammad al-Sisi, a former high official of the military who was closely affiliated with Mubarak, led the transition into the 2014 regime and seems to have frozen the political environment with his iron fist.

Finally, the year 2025 will probably mark the twentieth anniversary of the Iraqi constitution. The 2005 constitution was drafted and enacted under strong US influence after Saddam Hussein's regime was overthrown. The 2005 constitution was supposed to charter a new life for Iraqi society: an age in which international input would provide the legal, political, and economic support to end the cruel Saddam-centered regime and its sectarianism that uplifted the political and social role of the Sunni minority while discriminating against the Shia majority and fighting the Kurdish cause for self-determination and independence. In 2024, Iraq is still a deeply divided country, in which Kurds have

1 The first UN resolutions on the intervention are the following: Resolution 1378 (2001) / adopted by the Security Council at its 4415th meeting, on 14 November 2001, https://digitallibrary.un.org/record/452431?ln=en; Resolution 1383 (2001) / adopted by the Security Council at its 4434th meeting, on 6 December 2001, https://digitallibrary.un.org/record/454021?ln=en; Resolution 1386 (2001) / adopted by the Security Council at its 4443rd meeting, on 20 December 2001. https://digitallibrary.un.org/record/454998?ln=en.

2 Agreement for Bringing Peace to Afghanistan between the Islamic Emirate of Afghanistan Which Is Not Recognized by the United States as a State and Is Known as the Taliban and the United States of America, February 29, 2020, https://www.state.gov/wp-content/uploads/2020/02/Agreement-For-Bringing-Peace-to-Afghanistan-02.29.20.pdf, https://perma.cc/3PZ5-YRJJ.

been able to carve out significant autonomy and Sunnis are left at the margins of an overwhelmingly Shia political environment.[3]

The political tensions that characterize Afghanistan, Egypt, and Iraq and the Middle East nations as a whole have been reflected in horrendous crimes and intentional or unintended ethnic or religious cleansings that have transformed the demographics in the region. Some consider Christians "the most vulnerable of religious groups in the Middle East;"[4] they certainly are the believers for whom the largest amount of data is available. Although this faith was born in the Middle East, it is on the brink of vanishing from it. Christians were once 20 percent of the total population in the Middle East; now they are less than 5 percent of it.[5]

Numerous factors have certainly triggered persecutions and contributed to the decline and displacement of minorities in the region. The most noticeable factor is ISIS and its systematic policy of ethnic cleansing,[6] which left Iraqi Christians "close to extinction."[7] But ISIS is not the only one to blame for the dire situation of Christians in Iraq. A 2019 report noted that while ISIS largely vanished, many Iranian-backed Shia militias who helped topple Saddam Hussein's regime and stabilize the country seem to have turned against Christians.[8] The Chaldean patriarch of Baghdad, Louis Sako, still warned in 2022 that Chris-

---

3 Philip G. Roeder, "Decentralization to Manage Identity Conflicts," in *Federalism and Decentralization in the Contemporary Middle East and North Africa*, ed. Aslı Ümmühan Bali and Omar Dajani (Cambridge: Cambridge University Press, 2022), 25; Ali al-Mawlawi, "Salvaging State Legitimacy in Iraq through Decentralization," in Bali and Dajani, *Federalism and Decentralization in the Contemporary Middle East and North Africa*, 120.

4 Philip Mounstephen, "Bishop of Truro's Independent Review for the Foreign Secretary of FCO Support for Persecuted Christians: Final Report and Recommendations," British Asian Christian Association, 2019, 26, https://www.britishasianchristians.org/baca-news/bishop-of-truros-independent-review-for-the-foreign-secretary-of-fco-support-for-persecuted-christians-final-report-and-recommendations/.

5 Joe Carter, "5 Facts About Persecution of Christians in the Middle East and North Africa," Ethics & Religious Liberty Commission, May 31, 2019, https://erlc.com/resource/5-facts-about-persecution-of-christians-in-the-middle-east-and-north-africa/. Other statistics suggest that the Christian population in the Middle East declined from 6,1 percent in 1970 to 4,2 percent in 2020. Deanna Ferree Womack, "Christian Communities in the Contemporary Middle East: An Introduction," *Exchange* 49, nos. 3–4 (2020): 189, 196.

6 Erica C. D. Hunter, "Persecution of Christians by Isis Contradicts Idea of a Caliphate," The Conversation, July 28, 2014, https://theconversation.com/persecution-of-christians-by-isis-contradicts-idea-of-a-caliphate-29710.

7 Frank Gardner, "Iraq's Christians 'Close to Extinction,'" BBC, May 23, 2019, https://www.bbc.com/news/world-middle-east-48333923.

8 Mounstephen, "Bishop of Truro's Independent Review for the Foreign Secretary of FCO Support for Persecuted Christians," 58–59.

tians in Iraq "may soon disappear."[9] In the summer of 2023 Patriarch Sako himself left Baghdad for Irbil, in the Iraqi Kurdistan, after the government withdrew the decree that officially recognized him as the head of the Chaldean Church.[10]

In Afghanistan, the persecution of Christians that started with the Taliban in the 1990s never ended.[11] The Taliban government does not even acknowledge the presence of 0,2 percent Christians on the country's territory.[12] In Syria, there were 1.7 million Christians in 2011 and under 450,000 in 2019;[13] the city of Aleppo once had 360,000 Christian residents, but in 2019 the number was down to 25,000.[14] And where Christians have not been wiped out, they still suffer grave threats, such as the bombing of religious sites and the destruction of properties of the Coptic community in Egypt.[15] In Israel/Palestine, the downfall of Christian presence is "tremendous:" in 1922, Bethlehem was 84 percent Christian; in 2021 the number dwindled to 28 percent; similarly, Beit Jala went from 99 to 61 percent Christian during the same time period.[16]

The scenario is not just saddening for Christians, of course. In Iraq, ISIS slaughtered the Yazidis.[17] The Shia suffer attacks from the Sunni minority in Iraq[18] and Sunni extremists in Afghanistan.[19]

The disappointing outlook calls into question the efforts of many who have tried to instill a culture of rights centered on the rule of law in the region. The idea that the rule of law and other core values of constitutionalism would be the recipe for the Middle East and other jurisdictions has in fact pervaded

---

9 Lisa Zengarini, "Cardinal Sako Warns Christians in Iraq Risk Disappearing," Vatican News, August 24, 2022, https://www.vaticannews.va/en/church/news/2022-08/cardinal-sako-warns-christians-in-iraq-risk-disappearing.html.

10 Azhi Rasul, "Chaldean Patriarch Leaves Baghdad for Kurdistan," Rudan, July 15, 2023, https://www.rudaw.net/english/middleeast/iraq/150720231.

11 Eric Patterson, "How Did We Get Here? Religious Freedom Never Took Off in Afghanistan," *Cornerstone Forum* (blog), August 27, 2021, 1, https://religiousfreedominstitute.org/how-did-we-get-here-religious-freedom-never-took-off-in-afghanistan/.

12 Aid to the Church in Need, "Afghanistan," in *Religious Freedom Report 2023*, https://acninternational.org/religiousfreedomreport/reports/country/2023/Afghanistan.

13 Carter, "5 Facts About Persecution of Christians in the Middle East and North Africa."

14 Mounstephen, "Bishop of Truro's Independent Review for the Foreign Secretary of FCO Support for Persecuted Christians," 26.

15 Mounstephen, 18; "Christianity in the Middle East: Report 1," Christianity in the Middle East, 2021, 4, http://www.christianitymiddleeast.gr/publications/reports/367-christianity-in-the-middle-east-cme-report-no-1.

16 "Christianity in the Middle East," 13.

17 Huma Haider, "The Persecution of Christians in the Middle East," Institute of Development Studies, K4D Report 042, February 16, 2017, 11, https://www.ids.ac.uk/publications/the-persecution-of-christians-in-the-middle-east/.

18 Aid to the Church in Need, "Iraq," in *Religious Freedom Report 2023*, https://acninternational.org/religiousfreedomreport/reports/country/2023/iraq.

19 Aid to the Church in Need, "Iraq."

the narrative of rights of the latest decades.[20] For example, then US president George H. W. Bush made a very explicit statement on the topic at an early stage of this series of attempts to make the rule of law flourish in the Middle East. While addressing the US Senate to explain why the US military would intervene in the Iraq-Kuwait struggle in 1990, he said: "And today that new world is struggling to be born. A world quite different from the one we've known. A world where the rule of law supplants the rule of the jungle. A world in which nations recognize the shared responsibility for freedom and justice. A world where the strong respect the rights of the weak."[21]

President Bush's 1990 statement reflects not only his view but that of many who have been supportive of regime changes. Noah Feldman, who actively participated in the reconstruction of Iraqi institutions after the invasion in 2003, saw himself as participating in "a strategy of nation building aimed at creating democratically legitimate states that would treat their citizens with dignity and respect, and in which political change could be brought about via party politics, not extralegal violence."[22] "In short," Feldman wrote, "the objective of nation building ought to be the creation of reasonably legitimate, reasonably liberal democracies."[23]

Such high expectations do not seem to be merely a new form of imperialism disguised in humanitarian narratives, as some have argued.[24] There is scattered evidence of a widespread belief that, as does the rest of the world, the Middle East should enjoy the benefits of "a free society,"[25] namely a polity governed by a sound constitutional framework that contemplates a list of rights, the separation of powers, and, more fundamentally, the rule of law[26] as the "antithesis of arbitrary rule."[27] These features have characterized many endeavors in the

---

20 Among many, see Rosalind Dixon, *Responsive Judicial Review: Democracy and Dysfunction in the Modern Age* (New York: Oxford University Press, 2022), 66.

21 "Confrontation in the Gulf: Transcript of President's Address to Joint Session of the Congress," *New York Times*, September 12, 1990, A20, https://www.nytimes.com/1990/09/12/us/confrontation-gulf-transcript-president-s-address-joint-session-congress.html.

22 Noah Feldman, *What We Owe Iraq: War and the Ethics of Nation Building* (Princeton: Princeton University Press, 2006), 17.

23 Feldman, *What We Owe Iraq*, 8.

24 Michael Ignatieff, *Empire Lite: Nation-Building in Bosnia, Kosovo and Afghanistan* (London: Vintage, 2003).

25 David R. Stras, "What My Grandparents' Experiences in the Holocaust Taught Me about the First Amendment," *New York University Journal of Law and Liberty* 15, no. 2 (2022): 477.

26 Stras, "What My Grandparents' Experiences in the Holocaust Taught Me about the First Amendment," 485.

27 Dieter Grimm, "Levels of the Rules of Law on the Possibility of Exporting a Western Achievement," *European-Asian Journal of Law and Governance* 1, no. 1 (2011): 5.

1990s and 2000s, pushing or encouraging war-torn societies to embrace the rule of law with the goal of becoming liberal democracies.[28]

Paradoxically, the good intentions were probably counterproductive. International interventions and support aimed at instilling a legal culture that would protect fundamental rights—including religious freedom—through the rule of law were not just ineffective; sometimes regime changes or even just the prospect of them worsened the conditions of the local minorities, while the returns of dictatorships and illiberal constitutions brought them some relief. In Syria, Christians are now said to "be breathing a small sigh of relief" because President Bashar Assad regained control of much of the territory.[29] After the ousting of Mubarak and years of turmoil, the Coptic Church in Egypt has hailed al-Sisi's presidency and his strongman approach to power.[30] The starting point against which the exodus of Iraqi Christians is often measured is 2003, when Saddam Hussein's regime came to an end. In 2003, when the US-led coalition invaded Iraq, the Christian community was composed of some 1,500,000 members; now it has dwindled by 83 percent and comprises only 250,000 individuals.[31] Among them, with the exclusion of religious leaders, many believe that they should resort to self-defense rather than rely on the state army, and support the creation of a Christian militia to defend themselves, especially against Iran-backed security forces.[32] More broadly, it is widely believed that the American-led coalition that overthrew Hussein contributed to a climate of religious intolerance that culminated in ethnic cleansing in the early twenty-first century.[33] In retrospect, Noah Feldman confessed that "[i]nvading Iraq, in 2003, defeating and then disbanding the Iraqi army, created in Iraq a weak state—or maybe no state at all—in lieu of the strong one that had existed. The invasion and its aftermath thereby inaugurated a rich, new potential breeding environment for terror."[34]

---

28 Or Avi-Guy, "Transformation—Overcoming the Limits of Liberal Peace and Transitional Justice in Deeply Divided Societies: Reconciliation in Liberal Peace Theory," *Israel Law Review* 54, no. 3 (2021): 289. See also Judith N. Shklar, "Political Theory and The Rule of Law," in *The Rule of Law: Ideal or Ideology*, ed. Allan C. Hutchinson and Patrick J. Monahan (Toronto: Carswell, 1987), 16.

29 Gardner, "Iraq's Christians 'Close to Extinction.'"

30 "Christianity in the Middle East," 4.

31 Stras, "What My Grandparents' Experiences in the Holocaust Taught Me about the First Amendment," 477.

32 "Christianity in the Middle East," 27.

33 Mariz Tadros, "Religious Equality and Freedom of Religion or Belief: International Development's Blindspot," *Review of Faith and International Affairs* 20, no. 2 (2022): 102.

34 Feldman, *What We Owe Iraq*, 13.

As the Anglican bishop of Truro emphasized in his detailed report on anti-Christian persecution around the world, "[t]he 2011 'Arab Spring' and the fall of old dictatorships gave ground to religious extremism that increased greatly the pressures upon and persecutions of Christians in Egypt, Syria, Iraq and Libya."[35] Overall, it is widely believed that the end of dictatorships in the Middle East also marked the end of the protection that they granted minorities for years and even decades,[36] to the extent that religious minorities seem to welcome rather than oppose the return of autocratic figures to the political scene.

Scholars have often tried to explain the disappointing outcomes of so many attempts to spread the ideal of the rule of law in the Middle East, focusing on the details of the international interventions or the development of autochthonous constitution-building processes.[37] The main critiques have targeted the specifics of the American-led regime change in Iraq[38] and the often conflicting geopolitical strategies pursued by many of the participants in the international intervention to post-Taliban Afghanistan,[39] which ultimately resulted in the constitutional breakdown of the two countries.[40] More recently, some have also blamed the United States' pace and withdrawal process from Afghanistan.[41] Many critics have also stigmatized the calls of religious and ethnic groups to self-govern themselves after the end of dictatorships "at best as regrettable and outmoded forms of 'tribalism' and at worst as destabilizing

35 Mounstephen, "Bishop of Truro's Independent Review for the Foreign Secretary of FCO Support for Persecuted Christian," 22.

36 Haider, "The Persecution of Christians in the Middle East," 11.

37 Tofigh Maboudi, *The "Fall" of the Arab Spring: Democracy's Challenges and Efforts to Reconstitute the Middle East* (Cambridge: Cambridge University Press, 2022), 1; Sujit Choudhry, "Old Imperial Dilemmas and the New Nation-Building: Constitutive Constitutional Politics in Multinational Polities," *Connecticut Law Review* 37, no. 4 (2005): 933, 941.

38 Andrew Arato, *Constitution Making under Occupation: The Politics of Imposed Revolution in Iraq* (New York: Columbia University Press, 2009), vii–viii.

39 Tom Ginsburg and Aziz Huq, "What Can Constitutions Do? The Afghan Case," *Journal of Democracy* 25, no. 1 (2014): 119.

40 Bruce Ackerman, *Revolutionary Constitutions: Charismatic Leadership and the Rule of Law* (Cambridge, MA: Belknap Press of Harvard University Press, 2019), 18.

41 Among many, see, for example, Bret Stephens, "America's Crumbling Global Position," *New York Times*, October 26, 2021, https://www.nytimes.com/2021/10/26/opinion/us-military-russia-china-iran.html?searchResultPosition=2, or Katherine Schaeffer, "A Year Later, a Look Back at Public Opinion about the U.S. Military Exit from Afghanistan," Pew Research Center, August 17, 2022, https://www.pewresearch.org/short-reads/2022/08/17/a-year-later-a-look-back-at-public-opinion-about-the-u-s-military-exit-from-afghanistan/.

sources of disloyalty and conflict."[42] The main preoccupation has often consisted of assuring that Islamic practices and beliefs in Iraq and Afghanistan would not contravene the international standards of liberal democracies.[43] On the contrary, criticisms have hardly questioned the rule of law as the optimal solution for long-standing problems in the region. Some contemporary constitutional scholars have argued that the Afghan and the Iraqi constitutions of the early twenty-first century have gone very far in accommodating the religious component with the quintessentially secular constitutional culture,[44] giving life to the reality of a "*mixed system of religious law and general legal principles*," which would have become an "increasingly common approach to governing relations of religion and state."[45] It is debatable, however, whether such a mix adequately reflects and hosts the legal and political culture of the countries in which it has taken place.

The picture of the contemporary Middle East is so deeply disappointing that it calls into question not just the details or the results of years of financial, political, and military international—and especially Western—commitment. It calls into questions the goals: namely, the—implicit or explicit—association between democratization, the rule of law, and human rights on one hand, and the end of religious persecution and intolerance and the flourishing of stable and peaceful societies, on the other.

Within Western scholarship, some warned that not all societies would easily welcome and embrace constitutional engines designed elsewhere. In his 1990 study on democratic models, Arend Lijphart contrasted the Westminster model of democracy, in which a party alternatively wins at the ballot box and governs the country until new elections force it to surrender to another political platform, with what he called the "consensus model of democracy." He said that in heterogeneous societies

> [t]he policies advocated by the principal parties tend to diverge to a greater extent, and the voters' loyalties are frequently more rigid, reducing the chances that the main parties will alternate in exercising governmental power. Especially in *plural societies*—societies that are sharply divided along religious, ideological, linguistic, cultural, ethnic, or

42 Will Kymlicka, "Devolution and the Promotion (or Evasion) of Minority Rights," in Bali and Dajani, *Federalism and Decentralization in the Contemporary Middle East and North Africa*, 50.

43 Noah Feldman, "Imposed Constitutionalism," *Connecticut Law Review* 37, no. 5 (2005): 871.

44 Ran Hirschl, *Constitutional Theocracy* (Cambridge, MA: Harvard University Press, 2010), 35.

45 Hirschl, *Constitutional Theocracy*, 35.

> racial lines into virtually separate subsocieties with their own political parties, interest groups, and media of communication—the flexibility necessary for majoritarian democracy is likely to be absent. Under these conditions, majority rule is not only undemocratic but also dangerous, because minorities that are continually denied access to power will feel excluded and discriminated against and may lose their allegiance to the regime.[46]

Lijphart insisted that, in such societies, democracy would thrive only if it secured "consensus instead of opposition." The only viable democratic formula under these circumstances should pursue political inclusion and integrate as many interlocutors as possible into the political majority. He called "consensus democracy" this type of constitutional arrangement.[47]

Lijphart's statements seem almost prophetic for what happened in the Middle East. The mosaic of ethnic and religious loyalties has often resisted the implantation of majoritarian democracies that abide by the rule of law and a list of constitutional liberties in the region. The opinion of Lijphart or of those who followed in his footsteps hardly made an impact on how many devised the new Middle East that had to surface after the ousting of secularist or religiously fanatic dictators.

In this book, I explore why Lijphart's diagnosis and recommendations did not go very far. I argue that the reputation of the rule of law concealed the reality that the Middle East could not flourish simply by copycatting constitutional solutions from the West. In fact, the situation in the Middle East provides an opportunity to reflect on the limits of the rule of law as a universal ideal and machinery. The political, military, cultural, and legal efforts that international organizations, national governments, and academics have put into toppling local rulers and replacing them with sound governments that operate according to the rule of law may have failed to protect social peace and religious freedom when they have not undermined it. The belief in the rule of law as a universal or quasi-universal recipe with almost thaumaturgic qualities—"*the most precious human invention of all time*," in some wording[48]—stems from a series of preju-

46 Arend Lijphart, *Patterns of Democracy: Government Forms and Performance in Thirty-Six Countries*, 2nd ed. (New Haven: Yale University Press, 2012), 9, 30, 32–33.

47 Lijphart, *Patterns of Democracy*, 33.

48 Adis Merdzanovic and Kalypso Nicolaidis, "Advocacy for a Citizen-Centric Rule of Law Agenda: How Do We Bring the Rule of Law to Life?," *European Law Journal* 27, nos. 1–3 (2021): 298.

dices and the underestimation of the characters of the local legal and political tradition of the Middle East.[49]

I contrast the main constitutional characters of Afghanistan, Egypt, and Iraq with the paradigms of the rule of law, and argue for a more pragmatic, more realistic, and, one hopes, more effective approach to protecting religious freedom and religious and ethnic minorities.[50] These countries are particularly significant as Afghanistan and Iraq have been the main targets of international or western intervention, while Egypt experienced a series of autochthonous political attempts to entrench rule-of-law principles within the domestic constitutional setting. Despite the different circumstances that they have undergone and the strategies that were employed to break away from the previous regimes, Afghanistan, Egypt, and Iraq have not delivered on their promises. Afghanistan has failed in chaos, Iraq is plagued by highly weak and unstable government coalitions, and "[w]ith a revolution, a military coup, a counterrevolution, and two constitutions adopted in just two years, the Egyptian transitional process held the most dramatic series of events of the Arab Spring."[51]

Through a concise analysis of key political and legal institutions, I zoom in on the social fabric of these countries and how they have traditionally functioned. I contrast them with some key aspects of the rule of law—namely the ideal of individualism, the principle of equality, and the role of adjudication—and ultimately argues for a reconsideration of the rule of law and a better understanding of the political and legal environment in the Middle East. The rule of law is a demanding concept that cannot be easily exported. It is just one constitutional option, not the basic axiom for civilized societies—and certainly not the standard model for the Middle East.

I do not rule out the possibility that the demanding notion of the rule of law may successfully operate in the Middle East. Upheavals that demanded the respect of the rule of law in Tunisia—a North African country that shares many commonalities with the Middle East—were lucky, at least for a while.[52] But I warn against superficial generalizations that overlook some key aspects of political and legal scenarios that can greatly affect the success of rule of law-based projects.

I offer a fresh view of the trajectories that Afghanistan, Iraq, and Egypt underwent before and after their regimes were toppled. I test the observation of

---

49 Grimm, "Levels of the Rules of Law on the Possibility of Exporting a Western Achievement," 6.

50 Throughout the book, I use the English-language translations of constitutional texts provided by Constitute, https://constituteproject.org.

51 Maboudi, *The "Fall" of the Arab Spring*, 9.

52 Maboudi, 319.

Francis Fukuyama that, if modern statehood requires democratic institutions and the rule of law "[i]f there is anything that the experience of the past 25 years should have taught us, it is that the democratic leg … is much easier to construct than the rule of law"[53]—an observation that, Fukuyama added, Afghanistan and Iraq perfectly corroborated with their troubled constitutional and political developments.[54]

1 Religious Freedom and Religious Life in the Middle East

Introduction

Every year, the World Justice Project compiles the Rule of Law Index of just under 150 countries based on eight factors: constraints on government powers, absence of corruption, open government, fundamental rights, order and security, regulatory enforcement, civil justice, and criminal justice.[55] Venezuela occupies the bottom position in the 2023 edition of the index with number 142. Afghanistan is at number 140 (it lost six positions since 2021), Egypt fluctuates around number 136, while Iraq is among the few that are not even on the list. The Worldwide Governance Indicators of the World Bank measure the societal confidence in national institutions and their capacity to protect and enforce individual and property rights:[56] in the 2022 ranking of the rule of law, which spans the extremes of −2.5 and +2.5, Afghanistan (−1.7) and Iraq (−1.8) edge toward the bottom, while Egypt occupies the center of the list (−0.3).[57] Interestingly, in 2000, before international military interventions and the Arab Spring, the scores of the three countries were slightly higher. The poor ranking of such countries seems to confirm the widespread and long-standing belief that the Middle East lacks a proper legal and political culture.

The state of play of Middle Eastern jurisdictions was already disappointing to domestic observers of the nineteenth century. Khayr al-Dīn Tūnisī, one of the Muslim visionaries who advocated for the adoption of written constitutions in

53 Francis Fukuyama, "Why Is Democracy Performing So Poorly?," in *Democracy in Decline?*, ed. Larry Diamond and Marc F. Plattner (Baltimore: John Hopkins University Press, 2015), 14.

54 Fukuyama, "Why Is Democracy Performing So Poorly?," 15.

55 World Justice Project, "2023 WJP Rule of Law Index," accessed November 6, 2023, https://worldjusticeproject.org/rule-of-law-index/.

56 World Bank, "Metadata Glossary," DataBank, accessed October 23, 2023, https://databank.worldbank.org/metadataglossary/worldwide-governance-indicators/series/RL.EST.

57 World Bank, "Worldwide Governance Indicators," DataBank, accessed October 23, 2023, https://databank.worldbank.org/source/world-development-indicators

the Islamic world back then, worked hard to persuade both his co-religionaries and Westerners that Islamic lands such as Tunisia could benefit from the rising tide of constitutionalism and from a process of constitution-drafting.[58] A member of the Tunisian political elite that had gained significant autonomy from the Ottoman empire, Tūnisī was also knowledgeable about Europe. With his 1867 pamphlet, he argued that Islamic territories could learn from the West and align to its political and legal institutions.[59] Tūnisī rooted his theories in the Islamic tradition to persuade the Tunisian establishment "to accept a reformist policy not only inspired by Western experience."[60] He thus emphasized that he was treading within the spirit of Islamic tradition, while denouncing "the disgrace and the deficiencies in economic development and public policy" in the Islamic world, to recommend that Tunisia pay attention to the "aspects of the Frankish nations … which ought to be known."[61] When Tūnisī wrote his pamphlet, Albert V. Dicey had yet to popularize the notion of the rule of law.[62] Tūnisī thus could not draw on Dicey's theories or deal with most of the issues covered by Dicey in his book, but he certainly shared the Western view that the territories under the Islamic dominion were backward and in dire need of development.

Shortly after Dicey magnified the virtues of the rule of law, Max Weber characterized the legal arbitrariness with the metaphor of a "*Kadijustiz*:"[63] a judge randomly issuing rulings while sitting under the shade of a tree. He drew on the notion of *Qadi* (or *Kadi*) (judge) in Islamic law, to convey the idea of whimsical justice provided by an Islamic judge. The use of this metaphor was not isolated: it populated also English case law,[64] and was later exploited by Justice Frankfurt on the US Supreme Court.[65]

Decades later, justice and fairness in Islamic countries also had a tough time for John Rawls. In *The Law of Peoples*, the titan of twentieth-century political

---

58 L. Carl Brown, "An Appreciation of *the Surest Path*," in Khayr al-Dīn Tūnisī, *The Surest Path: The Political Treatise of a Nineteenth-Century Muslim Statesman* […], ed. L. Carl Brown (Cambridge, MA: Harvard University Press, 1967), 8.

59 Linda Colley, *The Gun, the Ship, and the Pen: Warfare, Constitutions, and the Making of the Modern World* (New York: Liveright, 2021), 328.

60 Tūnisī, *The Surest Path*, 43.

61 Tūnisī, 77, 73.

62 A. V. Dicey, *Introduction to the Study of the Law of the Constitution*, 8th ed. (London: MacMillan, 1915).

63 Max Weber, *Economy and Society*, vol. 2, ed. Guenther Roth and Claus Wittich (Berkeley: University of California Press, 1968), 806n40.

64 As cited by Patrick Devlin, *The Enforcement of Morals* (Oxford: Oxford University Press, 1965), 51.

65 Terminiello v. Chicago 337 U.S. 1, 11 (1949) (Frankfurter J., dissenting).

philosophy admitted that, for the sake of global peace and peaceful international relations, fully fledged liberal societies could coexist with decent legal orders that discriminated against their citizens but did not persecute minorities. He found a metaphor for his reasoning in a fictional country that he called Kazanistan—an Islamic state, of course. Kazanistan, in Rawls's mind, was an "idealized Islamic people" who did not know of the "separation of church and state." In Kazanistan, Islam was "the favored religion, and only Muslims can hold the upper positions of political authority." "[O]ther religions are tolerated," however, and "minorities are not subjected to arbitrary discrimination, or treated as inferior by Muslims in public or social relations," he specified. Finally, Kazanistan would be "organized in a decent consultation hierarchy."[66]

Finally, Fukuyama recently noted the failure of constitutionalism in the Middle East, putting most of the blame on Islam, which he regarded as "an obvious cultural factor that has gravely complicated the possibility of democracy in the Middle East."[67] Overall, great Western and non-Western thinkers of various generations have therefore shared the view that a predominantly Muslim Middle East would need Western lessons on what makes a political and legal society sound.

An obvious subject for such lessons would be the rule of law. The repeated attempts to instill a new institutional and legal framework in the region have taken different shapes, but have largely shared the goal of promoting the rule of law. They have materialized through intellectual partnerships, military operations, and political influences, giving birth to a variety of models and solutions. Among the several incarnations of this strategy, Part 1 focuses on the main constitutional characters and trajectories of Afghanistan, Egypt, and Iraq. All these countries are Muslim but host significant or even high religious diversity, and have drawn most of intellectual and political attention. Despite the different circumstances they underwent, their strategies to break away from previous regimes have failed in chaos, highly weak and unstable government coalitions, or new iterations of autocracies. All in all, skepticism toward the political and legal culture of the Middle East has more than a grain of truth, as the region does not seem to share some of the basic political and constitutional tenets of the modern West. However, such a legion of criticisms toward the Middle East has often failed to realize that the region is permeated with a deep-seated, sophisticated culture, which operates according to specific premises, whereas

66 John Rawls, *The Law of Peoples* (Cambridge, MA: Harvard University Press, 1999), 75–77.

67 Francis Fukuyama, *Political Order and Political Decay: From the Industrial Revolution to the Globalization of Democracy* (New York: Farrar, Straus and Giroux, 2015), 433.

most of critics have satisfied themselves with the superficial observation that Islamic political and legal culture seems to reject rule-of-law transplants.

In this section, I look at the social fabric of these states, how they transitioned from one constitutional regime to the next, and how their constitutional trajectories ended, laying the ground for a comparison between their political and legal culture and the one encapsulated in the notion of the rule of law.

1.1 *The Constitutions in the Middle East*

The most recent constitutional texts of Afghanistan (2004), Egypt (2014), and Iraq (2004) have followed the footsteps of rule-of-law theorists rather closely. The idea of charting a new course based on the core values of constitutionalism is on full display in the constitution of Afghanistan that entered into force in 2004 under strong international impulse:[68] "The state shall be obligated to create a prosperous and progressive society based on social justice, preservation of human dignity, protection of human rights, realization of democracy, attainment of national unity as well as equality between all peoples and tribes and balance development of all areas of the country."[69]

Afghanistan's 2004 constitution stated that "[a]ny kind of discrimination and distinction between citizens of Afghanistan shall be forbidden. The citizens of Afghanistan, man and woman, had equal rights and duties before the law."[70] Political process put all Afghans on the same footing: "The citizens of Afghanistan shall have the right to elect and be elected. The conditions of exercising this right shall be regulated by law."[71] While "[t]he sacred religion of Islam is the religion of the Islamic Republic of Afghanistan," "[f]ollowers of other faiths shall be free within the bounds of law in the exercise and performance of their religious rituals."[72] Finally, the 2004 constitution stated that national legislation could not contravene Shariʿa.[73]

The post-Arab Spring Egyptian constitutional trajectory that spanned three different constitutional texts also aligned with broader constitutional values. The succinct Article 1 of the 2011 constitutional declaration stated that "The Arab Republic of Egypt is a state with a democratic system, based on citizenship." Article 1 of the 2012 constitution stated that "The Arab Republic of Egypt is an independent sovereign state, united and indivisible, and its system is dem-

68 Ginsburg and Huq, "What Can Constitutions Do?," 117.
69 Constitution of the Republic of Afghanistan 2004, Art. 6.
70 Constitution of the Republic of Afghanistan 2004, Art. 22.
71 Constitution of the Republic of Afghanistan 2004, Art. 33.
72 Constitution of the Republic of Afghanistan 2004, Art. 2.
73 Constitution of the Republic of Afghanistan 2004, Art. 3 ("No law shall contravene the tenets and provisions of the holy religion of Islam in Afghanistan.").

ocratic." Article 1 of the Egyptian constitution, now in force, finally displays a strong commitment to the broader values of constitutionalism by stating that "[t]he Arab Republic of Egypt is a sovereign state, united and indivisible, where nothing is dispensable, and its system is democratic republic based on citizenship and the rule of law."

The 2014 constitution further states that "[s]overeignty belongs to the people alone, which exercises it and protects it. They are the source of power. They safeguard their national unity, which is based on the principle of equality, justice and equal opportunity between citizens."[74] The emphasis on equality among citizens is reiterated in the provision that "[t]he state ensures equal opportunity for all citizens without discrimination."[75] Although the Egyptian constitutional texts sometimes differ in substantial ways, they all require that state legislation comply with Islamic law.[76] Regarding religious freedom, the 2014 constitution boldly states that "[f]reedom of belief is absolute;" then it adds that "[t]he freedom of practicing religious rituals and establishing places of worship for the followers of revealed religions is a right organized by law."[77]

The 2005 Iraqi Constitution states that "The Republic of Iraq is a single federal, independent and fully sovereign state in which the system of government is republican, representative, parliamentary, and democratic, and this Constitution is a guarantor of the unity of Iraq."[78]

The Iraqi Constitution adds that "Iraqis are equal before the law without discrimination based on gender, race, ethnicity, nationality, origin, color, religion, sect, belief or opinion, or economic or social status."[79] It also proclaims that "[e]very individual has the right to enjoy life, security and liberty. Deprivation or restriction of these rights is prohibited except in accordance with the law and based on a decision issued by a competent judicial authority."[80] The constitution gives a special place to Islamic law and secures the compliance of national legislation with its tenets, but "guarantees the full religious rights to freedom of

74 Constitution of the Republic of Egypt 2014, Art. 4.
75 Constitution of the Republic of Egypt 2014, Art. 9.
76 Constitution of the Republic of Egypt 2014, Art. 2: "Islam is the religion of the state and Arabic is its official language. The principles of Islamic Sharia are the principal source of legislation." This provision replicates the Constitution of the Republic of Egypt 1971 Art. 2 (as amended in 1980), Constitutional Text of Egypt 2011 Art. 2; Constitution of the Republic of Egypt 2012, Art. 2.
77 Constitution of the Republic of Egypt 2014, Art. 64.
78 Constitution of the Republic of Iraq 2005, Art. 1.
79 Constitution of the Republic of Iraq 2005, Art. 14.
80 Constitution of the Republic of Iraq 2005, Art. 15.

religious belief and practice of all individuals such as Christians, Yazidis, and Mandean Sabeans."[81]

All in all, the aforementioned constitutional texts put citizens on equal footing, are indifferent to their religious or ethnic affiliation, sometimes give limited recognition to tribal affiliation,[82] and assign only a small role to the ethnic or religious makeup of the state: religious laws regulate the status of Christians and Jews in Egypt and Iraq,[83] while the Shia minority in Afghanistan could conduct its affairs according to the Ja'afari jurisprudence until the Taliban seized power in 20211.[84] However, these appear moderate deviations from the general rule, which sees constitutions according to all citizens the same treatment.

Trying to enforce the general principles and rules of constitutionalism in Afghanistan, Egypt, and Iraq has proven extremely difficult and has often ended in ethnic cleansing, sectarian bloodshed, and religious persecution. What follows is a sketch of the journey of such societies between the twentieth and the early twenty-first century and of their failed attempts to implement constitutional systems that resonate with the rule-of-law principles that have become so central in contemporary constitutionalism.

1.2 *Constitutions and Religious Freedom in the Middle East*

1.2.1 Afghanistan: "The Best Islamic Constitution" and Its Legacy

Joel, née Abdul Rahman and born in Kabul, joined Christianity in 1990 and took the name of Joel while working for a Christian nongovernmental organization that provided health assistance to Afghan refugees in Peshawar, Pakistan. After converting, Abdul Rahman first wandered Europe unsuccessfully seeking asylum. Once deported to Afghanistan in 2002, his family disowned him and his wife divorced him. He was arrested and charged with apostasy after the police discovered that he owned a Bible.[85] Only a declaration of mental unfitness released under strong international pressure and an escape to Italy saved Joel from being executed for apostasy.

Interestingly, his deportation and subsequent misadventures in Afghanistan took place after an international coalition had toppled the Taliban regime, and while galvanized ex-dissidents abroad and local ethnic groups coalesced and approved the 2004 constitution that was supposed to turn the page for the

---

81 Constitution of the Republic of Iraq 2005, Art. 2, second paragraph.

82 Constitution of the Republic of Iraq 2005, Art. 45, second paragraph.

83 Constitution of the Republic of Egypt 2014, Art. 3; Constitution of the Republic of Iraq 2005, art. 41.

84 Constitution of the Republic of Afghanistan 2004, Art. 131.

85 Sultan M. Munadi, "Afghan Case against Christian Convert Falters," *New York Times*, March 26, 2006, https://www.nytimes.com/2006/03/26/international/asia/afghan-case-against-christian-convert-falters.html.

country. The post-Taliban institutions that wanted him dead did not seem so different from the Taliban-led theocracy that he had fled years before.[86]

The territory of Afghanistan was slowly unified in the eighteenth century.[87] The British and the Russian empires fought over and around it for most of the nineteenth century,[88] until the British supported the centralization of power in a vast, fragmented, religiously and ethnically heterogeneous area to stymie the Russian expansion.[89] This process triggered a series of attempts to forge a predominantly Hanafi Sunni and Pashtu collective identity that ignored the Shia/Sunni divide, the multiple different rites and traditions within the two religious camps, and the Tajiki strong minority and other smaller ethnic and linguistic identities.[90]

The twentieth century did not bring real peace or stability to the country. The country has been governed by eight distinct constitutional texts between 1923 and 2004, with Soviets and Americans alternatively playing the pivotal role in influencing their drafting.[91] The Afghan constitutional texts of 1923, 1931, 1964, 1977, 1980, 1987, 1990, and 2004 did not dramatically change the reality on the ground, however.[92] Also the 1964 text, which was much in line with liberal constitutionalism[93] and was praised as "the finest formula for the reconciliation of Islam and constitutionalism in the Middle East to that date or since,"[94] failed to secure stability, order, and peace.

---

86 Andrea Pin, "A Constitution with Two Faces," Oasis, March 1, 2007, https://www.oasiscenter.eu/en/a-constitution-with-two-faces.

87 Nadjma Yassari and Mohammad Hamid Saboory, "Sharia and National Law in Afghanistan," in *Sharia Incorporated: A Comparative Overview of the Legal Systems of Twelve Muslim Countries in Past and Present*, ed. Jan Michiel Otto (Leiden: Leiden University Press: 2010), 273, 275.

88 Yassari and Saboory, "Sharia and National Law in Afghanistan," 273, 275; Faiz Ahmed, *Afghanistan Rising: Islamic Law and Statecraft between the Ottoman and British Empires* (Cambridge, MA: Harvard University Press, 2017), 6.

89 Clark B. Lombardi and Shamshad Pasarlay, "Constitution-Making for Divided Societies: Afghanistan," in *Constitutionalism in Context*, ed. David S. Law (Cambridge: Cambridge University Press, 2021), 97.

90 Lombardi and Pasarlay, "Constitution-Making for Divided Societies: Afghanistan," 97.

91 Pin, *Il* rule of law *come problema*, 150.

92 Pin, 72, 150.

93 Said Amir Arjomand, "Constitutional Developments in Afghanistan: A Comparative and Historical Perspective," *Drake Law Review* 53, no. 4 (2005): 945; Donald N. Wilber, 'Constitution of Afghanistan," *Middle East Journal* 19, no. 2 (1965): 216.

94 Arjomand, "Constitutional Developments in Afghanistan," 952. See also Shamshad Pasarlay, "The Myth of a Constitution's 'Goodness': What We Get Wrong about Afghanistan's 1964 Constitution," *International Journal of Constitutional Law Blog*, January 26, 2022, https://www.iconnectblog.com/the-myth-of-a-constitutions-goodness-what-we-get-wrong-about-afghanistans-1964-constitution/.

Although Islamic law does not contemplate custom as a source of law,[95] the Afghan territory has long been governed by an amalgamation of local customs and Islamic law.[96] Political institutions have combined tribal and ancestral foundations by mixing Islamic sources with local practices, as the only viable solution for a vast territory that comprises several ethnic, linguistic, and religious groups.[97] In fact, the vast majority of the Afghani population live in the countryside and demonstrate a strong cohesion around local religious authorities who also discharge public duties by reconciling local tensions and solving disputes in a nonjudicial fashion. Although the several constitutions of Afghanistan have often failed to recognize their prominent role or underplayed it, these local and tribal ties have not just played a strong local role; they have even affected the political transformations in the country, since tribal rebellions have often been the key factor in many constitutional changes.[98] Although "modernizers [have long] assumed that they could change Afghanistan by decree,"[99] the reality on the ground has therefore always consisted of leaders who exploit ethnic and religious affiliations, control portions of the territory, and mutually negotiate the public agenda both at the local and national level.[100] The Taliban regimes that ruled the country after the withdrawal of the Soviet troops and are in charge again now, despite their obsessive insistence on ruling on the basis of Islamic law, have also been heavily dependent on this logic.[101]

The 2004 constitution, which was drafted in Bonn, Germany, with the view of chartering domestic stabilization, did not reflect the complex reality of the religious, ethnic, and tribal loyalties that characterize Afghan society.[102] It cited the importance of the tribes among its opening articles[103] and contemplated "generous provisions" for ethnic, cultural, and religious pluralism,[104] including a personal status for Shias, whose population ranges between the 8 and the 15

---

95 Pin, *Il* rule of law *come problema*, 150.

96 Yassari and Saboory, "Sharia and National Law in Afghanistan," 273, 279.

97 Yassari and Saboory," 273, 279; Pin, *Il* rule of law *come problema*, 150–51.

98 Arjomand, "Constitutional Developments in Afghanistan," 947–48.

99 Thomas Barfield, "Afghanistan's Ethnic Puzzle: Decentralizing Power Before the U.S. Withdrawal," *Foreign Affairs* 90, no. 5 (2011): 58.

100 Barfield, "Afghanistan's Ethnic Puzzle," 56.

101 Barfield, 60.

102 Ginsburg and Huq, "What Can Constitutions Do?," 117.

103 Constitution of Afghanistan 2004, Arts. 4 and 6.

104 Arjomand, "Constitutional Developments in Afghanistan," 957; "2022 Report on International Religious Freedom: Afghanistan," US Department of State, Office of International Religious Freedom, accessed November 6, 2023, https://www.state.gov/reports/2022-report-on-international-religious-freedom/afghanistan/.

percent of the Afghans.[105] However, this text did not acknowledge the political relevance of tribes or clans and the quasi-judicial role that tribal groups have constantly discharged.[106] It even seemed to boycott the mechanisms that make sociality feasible, as it prohibited the creation of tribal parties that could respect and reflect the social cleavages.[107] It treated Islam as a common trait of the Afghan people but did not recognize the several and important identity markers that divided them.

By trying to free Afghans from their ancestral institutions, the 2004 constitution thus fought their social and political fabric instead of integrating it. The Western supporters of a free Afghanistan who had already misunderstood the national political culture after the Soviet Army left the country in the 1990s, unintentionally chartering the first Taliban rule,[108] thus made the same mistake again during the post-2001 constitutional process.[109] Local and ethnic affiliations played a growing role in Afghan society, absent any constitutional legitimacy or even against the spirit of the 2004 constitution.[110] The Taliban seized control of the country not just after the Soviets left, but also much more recently in 2021, with the opposite logic: they infiltrated the society by forming an alliance with the Pashtun majority of the population.[111]

After several years of Western involvement and partnering with the newborn Afghani institutions, analysts realized that a fully fledged statehood that would control the whole of Afghanistan was beyond reach. Some of them even suggested partitioning the country and leaving the south to the Taliban, whose links with the Pashtun tribes had not been severed.[112] Only in 2020, however, the United States, which had led the development of a new constitutional order, really came to terms with reality and decided to negotiate with the Taliban in Qatar, before ultimately leaving the country.[113]

---

105 Arjomand, "Constitutional Developments in Afghanistan," 957.

106 Massimo Papa, *Afghanistan: tradizione giuridica e ricostruzione dell'ordinamento tra Šarī'a, consuetudini e diritto statale* (Turin: Giappichelli, 2006), 314–16.

107 *See* Constitution of the Republic of Afghanistan 2004, Art. 35 ("Formation and operation of a party on the basis of tribalism, parochialism, language, as well as religious sectarianism shall not be permitted.").

108 Yassari and Saboory, "Sharia and National Law in Afghanistan," 273, 280–90.

109 Pin, *Il* rule of law *come problema*, 154.

110 Barfield, "Afghanistan's Ethnic Puzzle," 55.

111 Pin, *Il* rule of law *come problema*, 154; Conor Keane, US *Nation Building in Afghanistan* (London: Routledge, 2017), 33.

112 Robert D. Blackwill, "Plan B in Afghanistan: Why a De Facto Partition is the Least Bad Option," *Foreign Affairs* 90, no. 1 (2011): 42–45.

113 Agreement for Bringing Peace to Afghanistan between the Islamic Emirate of Afghanistan Which Is Not Recognized by the United States as a State and Is Known as the Taliban and the United States of America.

The 2020 Doha accords prepared the ground for the replacement of a failed, internationally backed constitutional regime that was supposed to implant the seeds of constitutionalism with a formally Islamic law system: the Taliban soon declared that the country, renamed as the Islamic Emirate of Afghanistan, would be run according to Islamic law, and that consequently no constitutional text was in force anymore.[114]

The Islamic Emirate of Afghanistan has not risen because it has left behind the complex web of loyalties that pervade the national culture. Despite its formal compliance with Islamic law, it owes much of its fortune and operates according to a complex web of tribal and ethnic customs. It has emerged because it leveraged its partnership with the Pashtun, which has an unsurprisingly overwhelming share in the composition of the government. Despite the promises of including minorities, of the thirty-three members of the government, thirty came from the Pashtu ethnic group.[115]

1.2.2 The Egyptian Struggle for a Civic State

Liberation is the English translation of the Arabic word *tahrir*: a perfect name for the square that has welcomed numerous political movements calling for radical change in Egypt. For more than a century, Tahrir Square has been hosting Egyptians calling for liberation much more often than celebrating it. It garnered its reputation as early as 1919, when its official name was still Ismailliya Square, when the Egyptians protested the British occupation. It was the place where other anti-British movements gathered in 1946 and 1951. Only after the 1952 Revolution that toppled King Farouk did it officially became Tahrir Square. In 1967, when Gamal Abd al-Nasser resigned in the aftermath of the national defeat against Israel, a crowd gathered in the square, calling for him to return. In 1972 it was the site of student protests; in 1977, citizens complaining against rising prices gathered there. By the time anti-United States and anti-Israel protests took place in the square, in the 2000s, its name had been changed to Sadat Square.[116] But the call for liberation was so appealing to Egyptians that they buried the new name, and in 2011, the whole world knew that the Arab Spring in Egypt had its epicenter in Tahrir Square. If the twentieth century was a whirlwind for Egyptians calling for liberation, the early twenty-first century would not give them real satisfaction: in 2017, after six more years of civil strife,

---

114 Pasarlay, "Afghanistan's Unwritten Constitution under the Taliban."

115 Aid to the Church in Need, "Afghanistan."

116 Menna Taher, "Tahrir Square: Where People Make History," Ahram Online, January 20, 2012, https://english.ahram.org.eg/NewsContent/1/114/32175/Egypt/-January-Revolution-continues/Tahrir-Square-Where-people-make-history.aspx.

Egyptian novelist Alaa Al-Aswany, who was in Tahrir Square among hundreds of thousands of his fellow citizens, stated that they had "left Tahrir Square too early."[117]

Egypt has always played a special role in North Africa and the Middle East. The most populous Arab country is at the crossroads of two continents; hosts both the well-respected Sunni institution of Al-Azhar and a sizable Copt minority that makes up roughly 10 percent of the population and 90 percent of the total sum of Christians in the country;[118] and has tried to find its way to modernity since the early nineteenth century. When Mohammed Ali gave birth to a semi-independent state within the Ottoman Empire, one of his first moves was to send talented students to explore and study in the West. Rifā'a Rāfi' al-Tahtāwi, with *The Extraction of Gold in Summarizing Paris* (1834), brought back to his homeland frescoes of Western modernity—including a translation of French constitutional texts.[119]

Later, the opening of the Suez Canal made Egypt a necessary partner for countries willing to play a role within the global scenario. In the second half of the twentieth century, its wars and peace with Israel greatly affected the political outlook of the region. The nationalist pose of its great post-World War II leader, al-Nasser, called the tune in several other countries. And, as noted above, more recently, the Arab Spring that started in Tunisia found its hotspot in Cairo's Tahrir Square.

Since 2014, the constitutional trajectory of Egypt appears to have stalled. A strong president of the republic and a mighty military power now shape the agenda and discharge the role of absolute playmakers. The clock seems to have gone back to the decades of Mubarak's presidency.[120] The state of play in Egypt finds its explanation at least in a decades-long struggle among the military, supporters of secularization, and pro-religion factions that collectively make up the country. None of these forces have been able to seize power once and for

---

117 Michele Giorgio, Alaa al Aswany: Young People Will Be the Leaders of the New Egyptian Revolution, Near East News Agency, April 8, 2017, https://nena-news.it/alaa-al-aswany-young-people-will-be-the-leaders-of-the-new-egyptian-revolution/.

118 "2022 Report on International Religious Freedom: Egypt," US Department of State, Office of International Religious Freedom, accessed November 6, 2023, https://www.state.gov/reports/2022-report-on-international-religious-freedom/egypt/; "Christianity in the Middle East," 4.

119 Rifā'a Rāfi' al-Tahtāwi, *An Account of a Stay in France by an Egyptian Cleric (1826–1831)*, ed. Daniel L. Newman (London: Saqi Books, 2004).

120 Abdul Ghafoor Saboori, "Parwan Governor, Citing Supreme Leader, Says Previous Constitution Invalid," TOLO News, August 4, 2022, https://tolonews.com/afghanistan-179259.

all, nor have the three agreed among themselves that a rule-of-law-based democracy would be the optimal framework for everyone.

In the aftermath of World War II, the rise of al-Nasser was marked by a threefold ambition. He insisted on the Egyptian "dignity" and on the need for the country to find its place among nations on an equal footing.[121] This magnified the importance of Egyptian citizens—Muslims and Christians alike—being on the same footing as proud members of the same political order. Second, his political assertion combined with a strong emphasis on the public role of the army, which entailed the militarization of the society.[122] Finally, following a tendency that already surfaced in the Ottoman Empire in the nineteenth century, Egypt set out to secularize its law, moving it away from religious institutions.[123] The great legal scholar Abd al-Razzāq al-Sanhūrī, who had studied for his doctorate in Lyon, was of the view that Egypt needed to root itself deeper into the hearts of its citizens through a new legal infrastructure, as France and Italy had done when they wanted to establish themselves as modern nation states.[124]

Al-Sanhūrī thought that it would not be possible to transform the legal institutions of the country into a fully-fledged Western system, uprooting Islamic law. He envisioned the Egyptian road *toward* Westernization as a series of incremental steps.[125] First, Islamic law had to become state law. Religious sources had to be replaced with state legal sources. The Egyptians would thus live by the same rules that operated for centuries, at least for a while. The nationalization of religious law would later trigger the nationalization of the judiciary: state courts and secularly trained judges would take the place of religious courts and religious judges.[126] These phenomena would gradually innovate the interpretation of Islamic law and pave the way for a further modernization of legal texts.[127]

121 Adeed Dawisha, *The Second Arab Awakening: Revolution, Democracy, and the Islamist Challenge from Tunis to Damascus* (New York: Norton, 2013), 54.

122 'Ala al-Aswani, *La dittatura: racconto di una syndrome*, trans. Giancarlo Carlotti (Milan: Feltrinelli, 2020), 14.

123 Mohammad Fadel, "Al-Qadi," in *The Oxford Handbook of Islamic Law*, ed. Anver M. Emon and Rumee Ahmed (Oxford: Oxford University Press, 2018), 319.

124 Samy A. Ayoub, "A Theory of a State? How Civil Law Ended Legal Pluralism in Egypt," *Journal of Law and Religion* 37, no. 1 (2022): 136, 145.

125 Enid Hill, "Al-Sanhuri and Islamic Law: The Place and Significance of Islamic Law in the Life and Work of 'Abd al-Razzaq Ahmad al-Sanhuri, Egyptian Jurist and Scholar, 1895–1971" [Part II], *Arab Law Quarterly* 3, no. 2 (1988): 185.

126 Ayoub, "A Theory of a State?," 147, 150.

127 Nathan J. Brown, *The Rule of Law in the Arab World: Courts in Egypt and the Gulf* (Cambridge: Cambridge University Press, 1997), 64.

Al-Sanhūrī did not see his plans come true. Islamic law never subsided, at least from a formal point of view. But Egypt gradually marginalized religious courts in the twentieth century, until religious courts were shut down for good in 1955. Meanwhile, the state took over the legal education of judges, whose legal culture drew inspiration from the West rather than from Middle Eastern legal traditions.[128]

The forced modernization of Egypt sought a middle ground between its military and authoritarian components. While its legal institutions were Westward-looking, and a culture centered on the principle of liberal constitutionalism was building, its strong leadership and its heavily militarized administration retained much of the power. Between 1952 and 2011, all the heads of the state were from the military and reserved a central role for themselves and the military. Meanwhile, although Egypt never broke away from the Islamic tradition, Islamic law certainly occupied a secondary role in the institutional and legal makeup. Al-Nasser himself made all efforts to sideline Muslim clerics and subdue Islamic institutions, also in an attempt to silence the dissident Islamic voices, such as those of prominent critics of Westernization like Hassan al-Banna and Sayyd Qutb, who saw the Egyptian drift away from Islamic law as a political mistake and as a civil treason.[129]

The financial and military failures between the 1950s and 1970s frustrated Egyptians and the promises of Westernization, sealing the fate of nationalism.[130] In the view of growing numbers of citizens, the poor economic and social results of the modernization of Egypt called for the reinstatement of Islamic institutions at the center of society and law.[131] The Muslim Brotherhood, the Islamic political movement that Hasan al-Banna had founded, rose as a political alternative.

Marwan Sadat, who had replaced al-Nasser at his death in 1970, tried to secure popular support and mitigate the critiques of the supporters of the Islamization of society by reinforcing the constitutional role of Shariʿa. Article 2 of the 1971 constitution had already made Islamic law one of the "sources of legislation;" a constitutional amendment in 1980 made it "the principal source of legislation." However, what Sadat achieved was very different from what he envisioned: Instead of assuaging Islamic voices, he pushed the compliance of

128 Brown, *The Rule of Law in the Arab World*, 23.

129 Albert Hourani, *Storia dei popoli arabi* (Milan: Mondadori, 1991), 442–43.

130 Al-Aswani and Carlotti, *La dittatura racconto di una sindrome*, 17.

131 Ahmet T. Kuru, *Islam, Authoritarianism, and Underdevelopment: A Global and Historical Comparison* (New York: Cambridge University Press, 2019), 28.

Islamic law further at the top of the political agenda, making the respect of Shariʿa a permanent feature of the Egyptian political and legal makeup.

Things did not change in 1981, when Sadat was killed and Hosni Mubarak took his place. Coming from the military, Mubarak led the country leveraging the power of the army, bringing the country closer to the United States especially after the demise of the Soviet Union, pushing back against the Islamist camp, and protecting the Coptic Christian community.[132] Between 1981 and 2011, Egypt spiraled into political and institutional stagnation under a military-backed leader who brokered domestic peace among competing factions and provided some sense of safety to religious minorities.

Between al-Nasser and the Arab Spring, three competing forces struggled to seize power in Egypt: the military—from which state leaders were picked; the Islamist camp; and the supporters of a civil state. The constitutional structure did not formally sideline any of these forces. In fact, however, the presidents of the republic set out to crush the Islamists more than once,[133] and attempted to dominate the legal field through curtailing judicial independence.[134] Between 1952 and 2011, Egypt thus paid lip service to supporters of Islamic law who strove to give life to a fully fledged Islamic-law-centered country, countered the rise of Islamists,[135] and threatened the independency of judicial institutions, which were most aligned with a Western liberal culture and struggled to protect their independence.[136]

The post-Arab Spring constitutional phase in Egypt did not see these tensions fade. After people of profoundly different views gathered in Cairo's Tahir Square to protest years of corruption, forcing President Hosni Mubarak to leave power, in early 2011, a constitutional chaos ensued.[137] Islamists soon leveraged the popular support that they had progressively achieved since the 1980s and gained the prominence they needed to appoint as president of the republic Mohamed Morsi, a member of the once oppressed Muslim Brotherhood. A

---

132 "Christianity in the Middle East," 4.

133 Alessia Melcangi and Paolo Maggiolini, "Christians Navigating through Middle East Turbulences: The Case of the Copts in Egypt," in *Migrants and Religion: Paths, Issues, and Lenses*, ed. Laura Zanfrini (Leiden: Brill, 2020), 190.

134 Awad el-Morr, "The Supreme Constitutional Court of Egypt and the Protection of Human and Political Rights," in *Islam and Public Law: Classical and Contemporary Studies*, ed. Chibli Mallat (London: Graham and Trotman, 1993), 260.

135 Melcangi and Maggiolini, "Christians Navigating through Middle East Turbulences," 190.

136 El-Morr, "The Supreme Constitutional Court of Egypt and the Protection of Human and Political Rights," 260.

137 Amal Jamal and Anna Kensicki, "A Theory of Critical Junctures for Democratization: A Comparative Examination of Constitution-Making in Egypt and Tunisia," *Law and Ethics of Human Rights* 10, no. 1 (2021): 197.

like-minded assembly managed to issue an Islamic law-oriented constitution in 2012—an outcome that was met with resistance among the military and the supporters of Western constitutionalism, including the Supreme Constitutional Court.[138]

Morsi's constitution did not last long. An army-supported coalition ousted Morsi in 2012. The year 2014 saw the arrival of a new constitutional text. This document did not remove Islamic law from the legal framework, but it had a stronger Western orientation. However, the military had the lion's share of power.[139] One of its members, Abdel Fattah al-Sisi, soon became president of the republic and some amendments in 2019 reinforced his powers alongside those of the military.[140] As a result, the president of the republic now controls the judicial appointments, including that of the president of the Supreme Constitutional Court, which is vested with the power of judicial review of legislation.[141] The structure of the state has been militarized to an unprecedented extent.[142]

The 2014 constitution now in force with its 2019 amendments curbs the judiciary's prerogative and provides Egyptian citizens with different legal statuses. While Article 2 still stipulates that Islamic law is the main source of legislation, Article 3 states that "[t]he principle of the laws of Egyptian Christians and Jews are the main source of laws regulating their personal status, religious affairs, and selection of spiritual leaders."

Since it became a republic, the constitutional and institutional trajectory of Egypt has displayed an endless tension among the Islamic, the civic- and human-rights-oriented, and the military components of the Egyptian society. The several constitutional texts that have seen the light of the day and the institutional dynamics reveal how each side has tried to monopolize the political and legal framework, rather than create a pluralistic environment.[143]

The multiplication of references to rights and Islamic law has tried to persuade both globalized forces and Islamists that the new constitutional setting

---

138 Jamal and Kensicki, "A Theory of Critical Junctures for Democratization," 198; El-Morr, "The Supreme Constitutional Court of Egypt and the Protection of Human and Political Rights," 260.

139 Zaid al-Ali, *Arab Constitutionalism: The Coming Revolution* (Cambridge: Cambridge University Press, 2021), 46.

140 Maboudi, *The "Fall" of the Arab Spring*, 149.

141 Mohamed Elgohari, "Deconstructing the Relation between Law and Authoritarianism: How Law Consolidated Authoritarianism in Post-2011 Egypt," *Arab Law Quarterly* 36, nos. 4–5 (2022): 458.

142 Elgohari, "Deconstructing the Relation between Law and Authoritarianism," 461.

143 Jamal and Kensicki, "A Theory of Critical Junctures for Democratization," 203.

would protect and even reflect their priorities. However, such texts have not deescalated the tensions. If, between 1952 and 2011, strong presidential leadership mitigated the visibility of their opponents, the political confrontations have increased since the Arab Spring.

The political and ideological makeup of Egypt still comprises three factions—the military, Westernizers, and Islamists—that alternatively support military or civil powers, judicial independence, subservience to the state leaders, or the fragmentation of civil society along religious lines. At best, among two of these three forces there are tactical alliances that attempt to sideline their most dangerous competitor, as happened when al-Sisi seemed to the Western and liberal thinkers a better alternative than the Islamists.[144]

1.2.3 Iraqi Sectarianism and Saddam's Bargain

Chaldean Catholics—who number fewer than one million—belong to one of the first populations to embrace Christianity. Those who did not join the Chaldean global diaspora are still predominantly located in Mesopotamia and especially Iraq, where they have witnessed the entire historical trajectory that transformed those territories into a modern state. Their leader, Cardinal Louis Sako, went to live in a Kurdish monastery for months, and returned to Iraq only after negotiations and amidst tensions.[145] He left his flock after the Iraqi government withdrew its official recognition of the Prelate—a move that, Sako feared, would allow the state to dispossess the Church of its properties.[146]

Sako did not flee Iraq while dictator Saddam Hussein was ruling the country. He left in late 2023, years after a partnership of domestic dissenters and foreign states had joined forces, toppled Saddam, and gave life to what they hoped would become a democratic, rule-of-law-abiding, institutional system. However, the story of Cardinal Sako suggests that the new republican era may have made the life of one of its most ancient religious groups volatile. The post-Saddam regime seems to have even splintered it, as Sako claimed that the Babylon Brigades, a self-declared Christian militia, were an Iranian proxy.[147]

The constitutional trajectory of Iraq has suffered from the same disease that has affected Afghanistan, although in different forms. As an independent coun-

---

144 Jamal and Kensicki, 205; Rawls, *The Law of Peoples*, 433.

145 "Cardinal Louis Sako Returns to Baghdad," *Iraqi News*, April 14, 2024, https://www.iraqinews.com/iraq/cardinal-louis-sako-returns-to-baghdad/.

146 "President Ends Recognition of Chaldean Patriarch, Putting Christian Assets at Risk," *Asia News*, December 7, 2023, https://www.asianews.it/news-en/President-ends-recognition-of-Chaldean-patriarch,-putting-Christian-assets-at-risk-58782.html.

147 "Iraq: The Isolation of Cardinal Sako," Information and Analysis on the Life of the Church, February 4, 2024, https://fsspx.news/en/news/iraq-isolation-cardinal-sako-42239.

try, Iraq came into existence thanks to the international coalition that ruled the Middle East after the demise of the Ottoman Empire.[148] The state was a vassal of the British Empire until it became a republic in 1958.[149] Saddam Hussein was able to seize control of the country over the 1960s and then govern it with an iron fist.[150] Under Saddam's control, "[Iraq] was a dictatorial mockery of the rule of law," where "citizens ha[d] no recourse to due process" against political brutality.[151] Saddam formally embraced the socialist ideals of the regional Baʿath Party,[152] which was founded by both Christians and Muslims and put people of different religious denominations on the same footing. He and his army, however, developed a narrative along ethno-sectarian lines.[153] They isolated the Shia majority,[154] which has some of its holiest places in the Iraqi territory,[155] and similarly sidelined and repressed the Kurdish minority, which is predominantly Sunni and has long craved the establishment of an independent Kurdistan.[156] Probably because they did not represent a threat, Christians enjoyed some protection under Saddam:[157] they could not compete demographically with Shia[158] and could not aspire to territorial independence the way

148 See Constance A. Johnson, *Iraq: Legal History and Traditions* (Washington, DC: Law Library of Congress, 2004), 11.

149 Johnson, *Iraq: Legal History and Traditions*, 12, 21.

150 Johnson, 29.

151 Richard W. Miller, "Might Still Distorts Right: Perils of the Rule of Law Project," in *Nomos: Getting to the Rule of Law*, ed. James E. Fleming (New York: New York University Press, 2011), 265, 269.

152 Kamyar Abdi, "From Pan-Arabism to Saddam Hussein's Cult of Personality," *Journal of Social Archeology* 8, no. 1 (2008): 13.

153 Ahmed Hasim, "Saddam Husayn and Civil-Military Relations in Iraq: The Quest for Legitimacy and Power," *Middle East Journal* 57, no. 1 (2003): 34.

154 Alessia Melcangi and Riccardo Redaelli, "The Re-sectarization of the Middle East: Minorities, Communities and Identity Politics within the Current Geopolitical Confrontation," in *Protection of Cultural and Religious Minorities*, ed. Ida Caracciolo and Umberto Montuoro (Turin: Giappichelli, 2019), 117, 126.

155 Melcangi and Redaelli, "The Re-sectarization of the Middle East," 117, 126; Samuel Helfont, *Compulsion in Religion: Saddam Hussein, Islam, and the Roots of Insurgencies in Iraq* (New York: Oxford University Press, 2018), 36–51; Augustus Richard Norton, "Al-Najaf: Its Resurgence as a Religious and University Center," *Middle East Policy* 18, no. 1 (2011): 132.

156 On the episodic violent Baathist repression of Shia and Kurds, see Dominique Avon, *La liberté de conscience: histoire d'une notion et d'un droit* (Rennes: Presses universitaires de Rennes, 2020), 1004.

157 Anthony O'Mahony, "Christianity in Modern Iraq," *International Journal for the Study of the Christian Church* 4, no. 1 (2004): 128–29.

158 Christians numbered around 3–5 percent of the total population. O'Mahony, "Christianity in Modern Iraq," 123.

Kurds did because of their overwhelming presence in the Northern part of the country.[159]

The coalition that ousted Saddam Hussein in 2003 set out to develop a sound constitutional framework. As seen above, the 2004 constitutional text foresaw the birth of democratic institutions, within which individuals would vote according to their individual leanings and opinions and the elected bodies would negotiate in pursuance of the public interest. The reality was very distant from this picture, however. The demographically predominant Shia exploited the democratic mechanisms to rule the country according to their political agenda,[160] which vacillated between the interests of neighboring Iran and local Shia intellectuals.[161] Kurds traded their independence claims for a decentralized state that would secure great levels of autonomy and the exploitation of the rich oil plants of the Kurdish region.[162]

Sunnis did not simply lose power.[163] The constitution banned the Baʿath Party that Saddam Hussein once led.[164] Moreover, in trying to replicate the historically successful denazification of Germany after World War II,[165] the new regime removed large portions of the personnel from public posts to facilitate the beginning of a new constitutional and political course.[166] As the army was

---

159 Gilgamesh Nabeel and Saad Salloum, "Christians in Post-2003 Iraq: Fragmentation Dynamics, Ethnic and Sectarian Fault Lines," Centre Français de Recherche sur l'Irak, August 11, 2023, https://cfri-irak.com/en/article/christians-in-post-2003-iraq-fragmentation-dynamics-ethnic-and-sectarian-fault-lines-2023-08-11.

160 Feldman, *What We Owe Iraq*, 78.

161 Fanar Haddad, "Shia-centric State Building and Sunni Rejection in Post-2003 Iraq," Carnegie Endowment for International Peace, January 7, 2016, https://carnegieendowment.org/2016/01/07/shia-centric-state-building-and-sunni-rejection-in-post-2003-iraq-pub-62408; Romy Haber, "Fostering a Security Architecture for Minorities in the Levant: Failed Shots," *IACL-AIDC Blog*, October 20, 2022, https://blog-iacl-aidc.org/lebanon/2022/10/20/fostering-a-security-architecture-for-minorities-in-the-levant-failed-shots.

162 John McGarry and Brendan O'Leary, "Iraq's Constitution of 2005: Liberal Consociation as Political Prescription," *International Journal of Constitutional Law* 5, no. 4 (2007): 674, 681.

163 Donald L. Horowitz, "Conciliatory Institutions and Constitutional Processes in Post-conflict States," *William & Mary Law Review* 49, no. 4 (2008): 1230.

164 Constitution of the Republic of Iraq 2005, Art. 7 ("Any entity or program that adopts, incites, facilitates, glorifies, promotes, or justifies racism or terrorism or accusations of being an infidel (takfir) or ethnic cleansing, especially the Saddamist Baʿath in Iraq and its symbols, under any name whatsoever, shall be prohibited. Such entities may not be part of political pluralism in Iraq.").

165 Daniel Johnson, "What Iraq Can Learn from De-Nazification," *Wall Street Journal*, April 22, 2013, https://www.wsj.com/articles/SB105095981621579000.

166 James P. Pfiffner, "US Blunders in Iraq: De-Baathification and Disbanding the Army," *Intelligence and National Security* 25, no. 1 (2010): 76 ("Lustration policies not only reform the institutions but also punish the personnel involved in past violations by preventing them from the benefits of one of their constitutional rights, i.e., the right to hold public offices.");

led mainly by Sunnis who had been loyal to Saddam, it was largely disbanded.[167] Many of those who were left without a job and socially marginalized but had military training found an alternative in the rising ISIS and its ranks.[168] ISIS was able to pay high salaries to its troops and gave them the opportunity to fight the Shia, who, in their view, had ruined their lives.[169] The new Shia-led Iraqi army thus became the target of many Sunnis.[170] Or, in Noah Feldman's words, "some nontrivial number of Sunnis seemed to believe that the summed costs and benefits to them of subverting the emergence of a democratic government in Iraq outweighed the costs and benefits of entering into a democratic state in which they feared becoming permanent losers."[171]

In summary, despite the good intention of giving life to a constitutional state, the democratic experiment in Iraq probably started with Sisyphean task and soon became a sectarian chaos,[172] within which the smallest minorities, such as Christians, were the most exposed to violence, as they did not have the political leverage that the Shia now enjoyed, a military apparatus to defend a territory that was comparable to the Kurds, or ISIS's protection.[173]

In recent years, Iraq reached some stability through decentralization of power and the apportionment of public posts among the three main religious communities—Shia, Sunnis, and Kurds.[174] The ethno-sectarian lines mitigated by the 2004 constitution, which reserved some seats to religious minorities and left the choice between religious and civil courts in matter of personal status to their citizens,[175] have made a major comeback in the government.

Eman M. Rashwan, "The Price of Transitional Justice: A Cost-Benefit Analysis of Its Mechanisms in Post-Revolution Phase," *University of Bologna Law Review* 6, no. 1 (2021): 126.

167 See Mark Thompson, "How Disbanding the Iraqi Army Fueled ISIS," *Time*, May 28, 2015, https://time.com/3900753/isis-iraq-syria-army-united-states-military/.

168 Thompson, "How Disbanding the Iraqi Army Fueled ISIS"; Walter A. McDougall, *The Tragedy of* U.S. *Foreign Policy: How America's Civil Religion Betrayed the National Interest* (New Haven: Yale University Press, 2016), 14.

169 Thompson, "How Disbanding the Iraqi Army Fueled ISIS"; Jessica Hartogs, "ISIS Cuts Fighters' Salaries Due to 'Exceptional Circumstances,'" CNBC, January 20, 2016, https://www.cnbc.com/2016/01/20/isis-cuts-fighters-salaries-due-to-exceptional-circumstances.html ("ISIS soldiers earn[ed] between $400 and $1,200 a month, plus a $50 stipend for their wives and $25 for each child.").

170 James D. Fearon, "Iraq's Civil War," *Foreign Affairs* 86, no. 2 (2007): 3.

171 Feldman, *What We Owe Iraq*, 43.

172 Fearon, "Iraq's Civil War," 9.

173 Otmar Oehring, *Christians and Yazidis in Iraq: Current Situation and Prospects* (Sankt Augustin: Konrad-Adenauer-Stiftung, 2017), 13–14; Fearon, "Iraq's Civil War," 3.

174 Al-Mawlawi, "Salvaging State Legitimacy in Iraq through Decentralization," 123.

175 "2022 Report on International Religious Freedom: Iraq," US Department of State, Office of International Religious Freedom, accessed November 6, 2023, https://www.state.gov/reports/2022-report-on-international-religious-freedom/iraq.

The government coalition is invariably composed by twelve Shia, six Sunnis, two Kurds, and one of another minority.[176] This often-criticized system, which is called *Muhasasa Ta'ifiya* (sectarian apportionment) was already envisioned in the 1990s among Iraqi exiles as a necessary compromise; later it materialized as the only viable solution to stop the spiral of sectarian violence.[177] This system has not achieved the modernization of the country, does not assuage smaller minorities, and is certainly distant from the hopes of the international forces that intervened and toppled Saddam,[178] but it reflects the reality on the ground, as political parties and coalitions tend to develop along either religious or ethnic lines.[179] The dissatisfaction with this settlement and its inability to address fundamental issues of justice and reparation—more than 200,000 Yazidis are still displaced[180]—is deep, but it is probably outrun by the preoccupations that its disestablishment would bring about more social strife and even sectarian hostilities.

Conclusions

On a superficial level, the recent events in Afghanistan, Egypt, and Iraq seem to have little in common. Afghanistan saw foreign troops leave while the Taliban reconquered their country; in Iraq, Saddam's regime is over, and now Iranian political parties are at the center stage; Egypt did not experience foreign interventions and transitioned from one autocrat to another. Underneath the surface, however, there are some commonalities among these three legal orders that resonate with the deeply rooted legal culture of the Middle East.

The constitutional texts enacted by these countries in the twenty-first century largely incorporated classic rule-of-law principles. They strongly emphasized the equality among citizens, their respect for human beings regardless of their gender, ethnic, or religious identity, and granted everyone

---

176 Massaab al-Aloosy, "With Iraq's Quota System the New Government is More of the Same," Arab Gulf States Institute in Washington, November 15, 2022, https://agsiw.org/with-iraqs-quota-system-the-new-government-is-more-of-the-same/.

177 Toby Dodge, "Muhasasa Ta'ifiya and Its Others: Domination and Contestation in Iraq's Political Field," In *Religion, Violence, and the State in Iraq*," Project on Middle East Political Science, Crown Center for Middle East Studies, Brandeis University, October 2019, 40, https://pomeps.org/muhasasa-taifiya-and-its-others-domination-and-contestation-in-iraqs-political-field.

178 Toby Dodge, "Iraq and Muhasasa Ta'ifia: The External Imposition of Sectarian Politics," Foreign Policy Centre, November 12, 2018, https://fpc.org.uk/iraq-and-muhasasa-taifia-the-external-imposition-of-sectarian-politics/.

179 "2022 Report on International Religious Freedom: Iraq."

180 Aid to the Church in Need, "Iraq."

access to justice.[181] Their basic structure thus echoed the rule-of-law mentality that is typical of systems that emphasize the importance of liberty and magnify individualism,[182] where political institutions pursue common interests and courts hear complaints and redress injustices. They reflected the widespread belief, recently captured by Cécile Laborde, that "Middle Eastern and Western states share a structurally similar *secular* project—whereby the state pervasively shapes and gives form to claims of religious difference and equality."[183]

The disappointing results of the international efforts that tried to secure the rule of law in the Middle East have hardly challenged these beliefs. There is still a widespread view that such poor results stem from a constitutional and political regression that frustrated people's expectations. According to such analyses, failed states are a historical accident that is unrelated to the regional political and legal culture. The only autochthonous factor that works against the rule of law would be Islam and its legal tradition, which has been a frequent target of Western criticism among legal and political theorists.

Theoretically, the social fabric of the area would be compatible with the requirements of the rule of law requisites: the failures are explained by mentioning a series of exogenous[184] and endogenous factors, such as the prevailing religious tradition and some defects in the constitutional drafting processes, myopic military strategies, or imprudent political accelerations, which prevented the institutions of the rule of law from functioning properly.[185] As Laborde noted, if properly understood and applied as a "secular project," the rule of law could replace the pervasive religious political culture in the area.[186]

The rule-of-law logic around which Western constitutional regimes were developed may not fit Middle Eastern societies. Despite repeated efforts to West-

181 Constitution of the Republic of Afghanistan 2004, Preamble; Constitution of the Republic of Iraq 2005, Preamble.

182 Hossein Esmaeili, "The Nature and Development of Law in Islam and the Rule of Law Challenge in the Middle East and the Muslim World," *Connecticut Journal of International Law* 26, no. 2 (2011): 338–39.

183 Cécile Laborde, *Liberalism's Religion* (Cambridge, MA: Harvard University Press, 2017), 13.

184 For example, see Ginsburg and Huq, "What Can Constitutions Do?," 117 ("The successes and failures of the 2004 [Constitution of Afghanistan] must therefore be understood in light of exogenous economic, geopolitical, and strategic dynamics.").

185 David M. Beatty, *Faith, Force, and Reason: An Armchair History of the Rule of Law* (Toronto: University of Toronto Press, 2022), 74 ("[d]uring the last half of the twentieth century, the rule of law lost its sovereignty and authority everywhere in North Africa and the Middle East. Most people lived under military dictatorships or the rule of absolute monarchs.")

186 Laborde, *Liberalism's Religion*, 18.

ernize the Middle East,[187] such societies still seem to function according to significantly different rules. Trying to enforce the rule-of-law logic and its sterilization of religious, ethnic, and tribal factors has destabilized societies that historically developed along these lines.

An underappreciation of the religious factor and of the role that religion plays in such societies has had powerful consequences for those societies. As Adam Chilton and Mila Versteeg have recently shown, statistics suggest that one of the key factors that resist the collapse of democratic regimes is the protection of religious freedom.[188] Religious communities have often displayed a unique mobilizing capacity, which has more than once resisted authoritarianism.[189] Misunderstanding and dismantling the local social fabric, including the political role of religious communities, has worked against the new constitutional edifices: it has crippled the new regimes, making life under them extremely difficult, if not outright impossible.

The troubled constitutional trajectory of the three countries exemplifies how the rule of law cannot be productively simply replicated and reapplied in different constitutional settings; such attempts can even backfire, as rule-of-law institutions and mechanisms may act as irritants for those legal systems. Egypt has failed to provide a common framework that would host conflictual Islamists, liberal supporters of Western ideals, and the military. The international coalitions that ousted the regime and guided the transitions in Afghanistan and Iraq ignored or underestimated that the Taliban and Saddam had successfully seized power because they exploited social cleavages that had deep roots in these societies.

In the next Parts, I analyze some key features of the rule of law and how they relate with the Middle Eastern social, political, and cultural fabric. In Part 2, I sketch out the logic of the rule of law. Because of its long-standing influence in the field, I start with the understanding of the rule of law offered by A. V. Dicey and later developed by some of the main theorists of the twentieth century. Part 3 focuses on the institutional equivalents of the basics of the rule-of-law in the Middle East, thereby illustrating the gap between the rule of law and its regional counterpart. Because of the political significance of religious freedom and of religious groups, I devote special attention to them in the context of the rule-of-law theories and in the Middle East. I do not suggest the complete irreconcilability of the Middle East with the rule of law, but rather that rule-of-law

187 Brown, *The Rule of Law in the Arab World*, 29–30.

188 Adam S. Chilton and Mila Versteeg, *How Constitutional Rights Matter* (New York: Oxford University Press, 2020), 239.

189 Chilton and Versteeg, *How Constitutional Rights Matter*, 239.

projects should be understood as demanding much more than basic requirements. Such demands may sometimes clash with local institutions and mechanisms, and especially with the local understanding of religion and of religious needs, thereby jeopardizing instead of helping to charter new constitutional courses.

Borrowing from what Christopher McCrudden and Brendan O'Leary wrote in the context of human rights, the two following Parts warn against "a particular form of universalist, or 'difference-blind,'" notion of the rule of law. Such a universalist approach "is generally well intentioned, but it has the potential to jeopardize peace and human security."[190]

2 The Rule of Law and the Place of Religious Freedom

Introduction

The constitutional provisions from the Afghan, Egyptian, and Iraqi constitutions cited in Part 1 regarding the rule of law, democracy, and freedom reflect some of the basic assumptions of liberal, post-secular societies envisaged by Western thinkers. Constitutional emphases on equality among individuals, judicial protection of rights, and the irrelevance of tribal, ethnic, or religious belongings echo the belief that, in Jürgen Habermas's phrasing, states are inhabited by individuals who enjoy "equal freedom of religion under the proviso that they no longer barricade themselves within their religious communities and seal themselves off from one another."[191]

This proviso translates into the constitutional requirement that "[a]ll subcultures, whether religious or not, are expected to free their individual members from their embrace so that these citizens can *mutually recognize* one another in civil society as members of *one and the same* political community."[192] This requirement is a necessary precondition for full and equal citizenship, and ensures that "the fate of religious minorities no longer depends on the benevolence of a more or less tolerant state authority."[193]

The idea that individuals mutually recognize each other as members of the same polity on an equal basis and personally engage in public deliberations that shape public policies is a feature of contemporary constitutionalism that

---

190 Christopher McCrudden and Brendan O'Leary, *Courts and Consociations: Human Rights versus Power-Sharing* (Oxford: Oxford University Press, 2013), xvii.

191 Jürgen Habermas, "Notes on a Post-secular Society," *New Perspectives Quarterly* 25, no. 4 (2008): 22.

192 Habermas, "Notes on a Post-secular Society," 22–23.

193 Habermas, 23.

is rooted in the rule of law, at least since the seminal contribution of A. V. Dicey. Writing while liberalism and bourgeoisie ideals were prevalent,[194] Dicey distilled the connection between individualism, equality, and the unity of the jurisdiction in vivid terms: "[W]hen we speak of the rule of law as a characteristic of our country, [we mean] not only that with us no man is above the law, but … that here every man, whatever be his rank or condition, is subject to the ordinary law of the realm and amenable to the jurisdiction of the ordinary tribunals."[195]

There is a common thread that unites Dicey to the latest contributions to the notion of the rule of law, sewing together the focus on the individual with other salient characteristics of the rule of law. Within the framework of the rule of law, the individual is the epicenter of the entire web of social and political relations of contemporary statehood. As Oxford professor of constitutional law Nick Barber has noted, an individualistic approach often characterizes the principle of equality in rule-of-law-based societies.[196] Political institutions, and mostly legislatures, are supposed to transform the diversity among citizens into a collaborative task, which "reduce[s] the risk of 'groupthink' that can arise amongst those of a shared background." Barber further elucidates the distance between that "groupthink" and the type of mentality that constitutional states require by stating that "[g]roupthink arises where a group closes in on itself; its members push each other towards consensus, shutting out dissent."[197] On the contrary, in contemporary rule-of-law based democracies, elected bodies "help[] bring people together behind a decision even if they continue to disagree with it."[198]

Three factors characterize democracies centered on the rule of law: the individualistic approach; the principle of equality; and the role of rights, courts, and adjudication. I focus on the relationship between the rule of law and religious freedom to show how the Western conceptualization of the former has reinforced a specific understanding of the latter. I summarize the model of conso-

---

194 Judith N. Shklar, "Political Theory and The Rule of Law," 1, 5; Mark D. Walters, *A. V. Dicey and the Common Law Constitutional Tradition: A Legal Turn of Mind* (Cambridge: Cambridge University Press, 2020), 11, 27.

195 Dicey, *Introduction to the Study of the Law of the Constitutions*, 110.

196 N. W. Barber, *The Constitutional State* (Oxford: Oxford University Press, 2010), 53; Shklar, "Political Theory and The Rule of Law," 5; but see Will Kymlicka, *Liberalism, Community and Culture* (Oxford: Clarendon Press, 1992), 165. Kymlicka argues that the individualistic paradigm is inadequate to preserve diverse societies and make them flourish.

197 N. W. Barber, *The Principles of Constitutionalism* (Oxford: Oxford University Press, 2018), 162.

198 Barber, *The Principles of Constitutionalism*, 163.

ciations that surfaced in contemporary constitutional studies as an exceptional regime—one that compromises on the ideal of the rule of law with harsh reality under certain circumstances. Making group—and especially religious—affiliations politically and legally irrelevant and requiring that society function as a group of individuals who engage in relationships on a predominantly individualistic basis is a key feature of the type of constitutionalism that developed around the notion of the rule of law. The prevailing understanding of the rule of law does not consist only of a set of very broad principles and mechanisms; it is deeply intertwined with a specific public culture that permeates education and narratives about the body politic.[199]

I use Dicey's theories as a template to explore some of the key characteristics of the rule of law and its relevance to contemporary constitutional theories. Although aspects of the rule of law are traceable back to ancient Greece and perhaps even before then,[200] Dicey has certainly played a central—and controversial—role in the contemporary success of the notion of the rule of law. Dicey influenced further ruminations on the rule of law after he identified the rule of law as having three distinctive features: (1) legal stability and foreseeability; (2) the existence of one legal regime that equally applies to everyone and are enforced by the same system of courts; and (3) a set of rights that individuals can claim in courts.[201] Despite Dicey's primary interest in the British constitution, his influence has extended well beyond that jurisdiction, affecting the concept of the rule of law on a global scale. This is no surprise, however, as his theories crystallized earlier ruminations of prominent European thinkers, such as Kant.

2.1 *The Features and the Logic of the Rule of Law*

Most of the conceptualizations of the rule of law developed along three distinct lines: the *formalist* line, which found its main point of reference in Joseph Raz; the *substantive* line, which has its main theorists in Ronald Dworkin and Tom Bingham; and the *procedural* line, which has been espoused by Lon Fuller and Jeremy Waldron and also surfaced in John Laws's insistence on the centrality "of impartial and independent adjudication" for the existence of the rule of law.[202]

On a superficial level, the formalist approach seems to be the least demanding. As it requires that the law be just foreseeable and stable, it does not appear

199 Donald Bello Hutt, "Rule of Law and Political Representation," *Hague Journal of the Rule of Law*, no. 14 (2021): 7.

200 Raymond Wacks, *The Rule of Law under Fire?* (Oxford: Hart, 2021), 9.

201 Dicey, *Introduction to the Study of the Law of the Constitution*, 110, 114–17.

202 John Laws, *The Constitutional Balance* (Oxford: Hart, 2020), 24.

to require much from rule-of-law compliant states.[203] In fact, a great deal of thinkers—from Raz to Grimm—have openly been of the view that the "[r]ule of law in a purely formal sense is compatible with oppressive, exploitative and discriminatory legislation."[204] However, even the thinnest formulations of the rule of law embed some philosophical presuppositions and constitutional ideals.[205] In this respect, there is more convergence among scholars than one would probably expect, especially on three decisive aspects of the notion: the individual, equality, and the role of courts.

2.1.1 The Individual

The individualist approach unites a variety of rule-of-law theorists, regardless of their thick or thin understanding of the notion. The protection of the individual rose to the top of the rule-of-law prerogatives when Friedrich Hayek promoted "individualism" as an "antidote to the intellectual confusion" of his time[206] and emphasized the importance that "[w]ithin the known rules of the game the individual is free to pursue his personal ends and desires."[207]

The individualistic approach is certainly on full display among those who embrace a substantive approach to the rule of law, such as Lord Bingham. With his emphasis on rights, Bingham expounded an understanding of the rule of law in which individuals occupy a central place.[208] Alongside Bingham, Dworkin similarly espoused a conception of the rule of law centered on individual rights, around which he built much of his scholarship.[209]

Intellectuals grown in the civil law tradition and who do not subscribe to a particularly thick understanding of the rule of law, such as Dieter Grimm, have similarly noted that in rule of law societies, "[f]undamental rights are designed

---

203 Joseph Raz, *The Authority of Law* (Oxford: Clarendon Press, 1979), 213.

204 Grimm, "Levels of the Rules of Law on the Possibility of Exporting a Western Achievement," 8.

205 Rivka Weill, "Acontextual Constitutionalism and the Relationship between the People, Constituent Power and the State: On Nicholas Barber's *The Principles of Constitutionalism*," *Jerusalem Review of Legal Studies* 24, no. 1 (2021): 203.

206 Avon, *La liberté de conscience*, 116.

207 Friedrich A. Hayek, *The Road to Serfdom* (London: Routledge, 1962), 54.

208 Legal theory and legal philosophy have long debated the correct understanding of the individual, and many scholars prefer using the word *person* rather than *individual* to convey a more social and less self-referential conception of the human being. I do not aim to espouse or reject any specific theory, only to emphasize the central role and importance given to the human being vis-à-vis social groups of any kind.

209 Ronald Dworkin, "Political Judges and the Rule of Law," Maccabean Lecture in Jurisprudence, 13 December 1977, *Proceedings of the British Academy*, no. 64 (1978): 262. See Wacks, *The Rule of Law under Fire?*, 5.

to limit government powers in the interest of individual self-determination."[210] The nexus between the rule of law, rights, and individualism that Grimm emphasizes is also present in Jürgen Habermas, who linked the idea of the rule of law with the citizens' enjoyment of "an *appropriate* use of their public autonomy," which, in turn, presupposes "an equally protected private autonomy in their life conduct."[211]

Habermas rooted the individualistic component of the notion of the rule of law even deeper in European moral and political thinking when he identified the main sources of inspiration for his reasonings on the rule of law in Jean-Jacques Rousseau and Immanuel Kant. In fact, Habermas notes that the focus of the two philosophers on individualism enables "the addressees of the law" "to understand themselves as its authors."[212] By connecting the rule of law with Kantian philosophy, Habermas thus shows that the rule of law bridges several pillars of Western political and legal culture, and argues that its individualistic component permeates this notion at least since the contribution of Kant.

Habermas's considerations are hardly debatable. Kant famously considered human autonomy as the defining characteristic of human dignity when he stated that "nothing can have a worth other than that which the law determines for it. But the lawgiving itself, which determines all worth, must for that very reason have a dignity, that is, an unconditional, incomparable worth; and the word respect alone provides a becoming expression for the estimate of it that a rational being must give. Autonomy is therefore the ground of the dignity of human nature and of every rational nature."[213]

Kant's thinking encouraged the interpretation of human history and civilization as a process through which individuals have emancipated themselves, transitioning from heteronomy to fuller degrees of autonomy.[214] These interpretations have reinforced the identification of individualism with autonomy, making human beings the authors of their own lives.[215] Such narratives of hu-

210 Grimm, "Levels of the Rules of Law on the Possibility of Exporting a Western Achievement," 9.

211 Jürgen Habermas, "Constitutional Democracy: A Paradoxical Union of Contradictory Principles?," *Political Theory* 29, no. 6 (2001): 767.

212 Habermas, "Constitutional Democracy," 767.

213 Immanuel Kant, *Groundwork of the Metaphysics of Morals*, ed. and trans. Mary Gregor and Jens Timmermann (Cambridge: Cambridge University Press, 2012), 43

214 Avon, *La liberté de conscience*, 117.

215 Jeremy Waldron bridged the notion of moral and personal autonomy when he stated, "we may distinguish between *moral* autonomy, which is the capacity Kant is talking about, and *personal* autonomy, by which I mean a person being in control of her life, reflecting on how things are going, working out what to do with her life, and so on. ... Talk of personal autonomy evokes the image of a person in charge of her life—not just following

man civilization have invested the notion of the rule of law with a strong belief in human self-determination.

In Habermas's thought, the impact of individualism and self-determination on the political and constitutional role of religion has been particularly profound. He has argued that the role of religion, which served as the institutional and theoretical background against which political and constitutional infrastructures were constructed for millennia, was "not replaced by a different idea;" individualism triggered its replacement with "the *procedure* of democratic self-empowerment, which is institutionalized in the form of equally distributed subjective rights, so that it can be exercised by free and equal citizens."[216]

Traces of individualism can also be found in the scholarship of Raz, although he is unanimously regarded among the theoreticians who support the thinnest version of the rule of law. Raz admittedly argued that the rule of law requires little more than that the laws be prospective, open, clear, and stable.[217] He explicitly criticized substantive views of the rule of law, because these would have made the notion difficult to grasp, blurred, redundant, and even useless. In his own words, the rule of law is "not to be confused with democracy, justice, equality ... human rights of any kind or respect for persons or for the dignity of man."[218] He went so far as to say that the rule of law "says nothing about how the law is to be made: by tyrants, democratic majorities, or any other way. It says nothing about fundamental rights, equality, or justice."[219]

Interestingly, despite Raz's emphasis on the formal component of the rule of law,[220] his political philosophy was nonetheless clearly individualistic.[221] He warned that a sharp distinction existed between moral philosophy and political philosophy, as when he distinguished between liberalism as "a doctrine about political morality which revolves around the importance of personal liberty" and individualism as "a moral doctrine."[222] But, he noted, "[r]ights-based moral

---

inclination as it arises but choosing which of her preferences to follow, and not just for moral reasons but because of the sort of person she wants to be." Jeremy Waldron, *One Another's Equals. The Basis of Human Equality* (Cambridge, MA: Belknap Press of Harvard University Press, 2017), 106. See Michael Ignatieff and Amy Gutmann, *Human Rights as Politics and Idolatry* (Princeton: Princeton University Press, 2003), 106.

216 Jürgen Habermas, "Reflections and Hypotheses on a Further Structural Transformation of the Political Public Sphere," *Theory, Culture & Society* 39, no. 4 (2022): 150.

217 Raz, *The Authority of Law*, 215.

218 Raz, 211.

219 Raz, 214.

220 Raz, 214.

221 Joseph Raz, *The Morality of Freedom* (Oxford: Oxford University Press, 1986).

222 Raz, *The Morality of Freedom*, 17.

theories are usually individualistic moral theories."[223] In fact, "[h]istorically, liberalism and individualism grew together."[224] Raz himself clearly espoused the individualistic approach that, in his view, characterized liberalism.[225] Expounding on the virtues of individualism, he noted that "[i]n Western industrial societies a particular conception of individual well-being has acquired considerable popularity. It is the ideal of personal autonomy … The ruling idea behind the ideal of personal autonomy is that people should make their own lives. The autonomous person is a (part) author of his own life. The idea of personal autonomy is the vision of people controlling, to some extent, their own destiny."[226] "Autonomy is an ideal of self-creation," he concluded.[227]

Raz's argument in favor of autonomy is particularly significant at least on two different levels. First, it testifies to a widespread understanding of the rule of law as *quintessentially* or *normally* embedding a morality centered on the individual. Second, with his emphasis on the human strife for self-creation, Raz highlighted that the rule of law is not just geared to protect the individual—it aims to make each human being the *author* or his or her life. The rule of law thus binds the legal and political institutions with the goals of social, cultural, and political emancipation of the individual: a viewpoint that Hayek already espoused, when he affirmed that the rule of law in his view was a prerequisite for the creation of "new opportunities open to all."[228]

In general, modern constitutionalism has developed along the deep-seated lines of liberal thinkers and rule-of-law theorists that have largely espoused a fluid and atomistic conception of political societies.[229] As Kay Moeller has made clear, that conceptualization of political societies has shifted the focus from the government to the individual, bringing about a specific understanding of rights: "the point of rights," Moeller writes, "is not to *disable governments*, but to *enable individuals* to take control of their lives."[230]

223 Raz, 191, 198.
224 Raz, 17.
225 Raz, 203. See also Weill, "Acontextual Constitutionalism and the Relationship between the People, Constituent Power and the State," 103.
226 Raz, *The Morality of Freedom*, 369.
227 Raz, 370.
228 Hayek, *The Road to Serfdom*, 57.
229 Jürgen Habermas, *Morale, diritto, politica*, ed. Leonardo Ceppa (Turin: Einaudi, 2007), 105.
230 Kai Möller, "Two Conceptions of Positive Liberty: Towards and Autonomy-Based Theory of Constitutional Rights," *Oxford Journal of Legal Studies* 29, no. 4 (2009): 758.

2.1.2 Equality among Individuals and Groups

Regardless of its thick or thin understanding, within the rule-of-law framework, states consist of individuals who mutually recognize each other as peers and are subject to the same rules.[231] In states complying with the rule of law, the law "applies equally to all regardless of their social status, rank, class, political influence, creed, race, nationality or sexual preference."[232] The equal treatment of all the members of the same body politic as individuals makes their belonging to specific groups or circles irrelevant.

The constitutional theory that has developed around the rule-of-law paradigm often accepts moderate deviations from equality; but it usually does so in order to socially and politically include the members of minority groups who would otherwise be excluded from the full participation in the body politic.[233] Groups thus enjoy special protection because of equality concerns and as long as they are numerically and socially inferior, in order to avoid that the majority tramples on their rights.[234] As Michael Ignatieff points out, groups are not protected in themselves, but to further individual rights: "[G]roup rights are needed to protect individual rights … the ultimate purpose and justification of group rights is not the protection of the group as such but the protection of the individuals who compose it."[235] This approach is evident in the several condemnations by the European Court of Human Rights of the Bosnian attribution of seats on the basis of ethnicity:[236] in its latest instantiation, the court ruled that "treating groups differently" was admissible only "in order to correct 'factual inequalities' between them." Because "none of the 'constituent peoples' [of Bosnia-Herzegovina] is in the factual position of an endangered minority" such an ethnic distribution of seats and posts was untenable.[237]

The only membership that the rule of law accepts without reservation and even requires is the one that binds people together as participants in the

231 Wacks, *The Rule of Law under Fire?*, 17.

232 Wacks, 52.

233 Tarunabh Khaitan, *A Theory of Discrimination Law* (Oxford: Oxford University Press, 2015), 51.

234 Larry May, "Bystanders, the Rule of Law, and Criminal Trials," *Nomos*, no. 50 (2011): 241, 261.

235 Ignatieff and Gutmann, *Human Rights as Politics and Idolatry*, 67.

236 *Sejdić and Finci v. Bosnia and Herzegovina*, app. no. 27996/06 and 34836/06, judgment of December 22, 2009; *Zornić v. Bosnia and Herzegovina*, app. no. 3681/06, judgment of July 15, 2014; *Pilav v. Bosnia and Herzegovina*, app. no. 41939/07, Judgment of June 9, 2016; *Kovačević v. Bosnia and Herzegovina*, app. no. 43651/22, judgment of August 29, 2023. See Jens Woelk, "Opening Pandora's Box? On *Kovačević* and the European Court of Human Rights' Fundamental Criticism of the Electoral System in Bosnia and Herzegovina," *VerfassungsBlog*, September 1, 2023, https://verfassungsblog.de/opening-pandoras-box/.

237 *Kovačević v. Bosnia and Herzegovina*, app. no. 43651/22, judgment of August 29, 2023 (Fourth Chamber), Par. 61.

same statehood. Mutual recognition among members of the same body politic is considered a prerequisite for the existence and the survival of a political community,[238] which, in turn, is an institutionalized group of people that pursues "the *political* common good."[239] The logic that values all the members of the state and places them on the same footing as individuals simultaneously makes ethnic, religious, or cultural rifts legally and politically irrelevant. As Joseph Weiler notes, democracies require that there be a unified body politic: "[t]he 'demo' in the word democracy is not lexical; it is ontological: No demos, no democracy."[240]

In democratic states that abide by the rule of law, citizens have the equal right to participate in the democratic processes that form elected bodies, which in turn, are in charge of identifying and pursuing the common good.[241] In Habermas's thinking, the connection between citizenship, political participation, and common good plays a fundamental role, as individual autonomy morphs into "political self-legislation" through the legislative process.[242] Or, he continues, "there must be a *recognizable* connection between the results of government action and the input of the voters' decisions such that the citizens can recognize it as the confirmation of the rationalising power of their own democratic opinion and will formation."[243]

Equality among citizens requires that there be only one body politic and one legal regime for all. Societies are properly constituted only if they become one polity in terms of "territory, people, and laws."[244] Within the rule-of-law framework, equality among citizens and the unity of the body politic therefore mutually reinforce each other. Everyone is subject to the same legal regime because everyone equally participates in the same body politic. It is no surprise then that Habermas has warned about the necessity that "the political public sphere of constitutional democracies" preserve their "inclusive space for possi-

238 Richard Ekins, "The State and Its People," *American Journal of Jurisprudence* 66, no. 1 (2021): 51–54.

239 Ekins, "The State and Its People," 54.

240 Joseph H. H. Weiler, "COVID, Europe, and the Self-Asphyxiation of Democracy," in *Democracy in Times of Pandemic*, ed. Miguel Maduro and Paul N. Kahn (Cambridge: Cambridge University Press, 2020), 146.

241 Richard Ekins and Jeffrey Goldsworthy, "The Reality and Indispensability of Legislative Intentions," *Sydney Law Review* 36, no. 1 (2014): 65.

242 Habermas, "Constitutional Democracy," 778.

243 Habermas, "Reflections and Hypotheses on a Further Structural Transformation of the Political Public Sphere," 152.

244 Jiří Přibáň, "Imaginary of the Rule of Law and a Force of Societal Transition: Central and East European Lessons from European (Dis)integration," in *Rule of Law in Crisis: Constitutionalism in a State of Flux*, ed. Martin Belov (Abingdon: Routledge, 2023), 75.

ble discursive clarification of competing claims to truth and the generalisation of interests,"[245] and avoid fragmentation into "islands of communication."[246]

The idea of equality has both legal meaning and moral importance. As Waldron has noted while reflecting on the relationship between dignity and equality, equality under the law "purports positively to establish the fundamental equality of all human beings on a substantial basis and at a very high level."[247] Ignatieff has similarly stated that contemporary systems that recognize and protect human rights leverage "the idea of moral reciprocity: that we judge human actions by the simple test of whether we would wish to be on the receiving end."[248] Philosopher Andrea Sangiovanni has sewed together the moral and legal components of equality when he argued that treating people as equals both fleshes out a sense of mutual respect and grounds a practice of reciprocal recognition among individuals. For Sangiovanni, the role of equality is so important and pervasive that it can make the controversial and ambiguous notion of human dignity unnecessary.[249] All that is needed to ground and reinforce the protection of individuals, he continues, is the mutual recognition among peers that everyone is worthy of respect and subject to the same rights as a member of the same political community.[250]

Although academics disagree in how they frame the notions of individualism, equality, or equal rights, they seem to speak with one voice: citizens enjoy the same rights because they all belong to the same body politic, without the need of any group mediation.

2.1.3 Courts

The notion of the rule of law has consistently included a strong consideration of courts as the protectors of individual rights—at least since Dicey. He famously insisted on the unity of the jurisdiction as a hallmark of legal civilization, to the extent that he largely misrepresented the regimes in continental Europe to argue that the English system was the only one that was capable of according to everyone the same judicial consideration.[251]

---

245 Habermas, "Reflections and Hypotheses on a Further Structural Transformation of the Political Public Sphere," 166.

246 Habermas, 162.

247 Waldron, *One Another's Equals*, 194.

248 Ignatieff and Gutmann, *Human Rights as Politics and Idolatry*, 88–89.

249 Andrea Sangiovanni, *Humanity without Dignity: Moral Equality, Respect, and Human Rights* (Cambridge, MA: Harvard University Press, 2017), 72–73.

250 Sangiovanni, *Humanity without Dignity*, 72–73.

251 Peter W. Hogg and Cara F. Zwibel, "The Rule of Law in the Supreme Court of Canada," *University of Toronto Law Review* 55, no. 3 (2005): 716.

Those who followed Dicey took the concept of the rule of law in different directions, but nonetheless gave prominent importance to the judicial process. As "justice is in the end a matter of individual right," said Dworkin,[252] courts are an essential aspect of the rule of law, as they have the power to hear individual claims of rights.[253] Lord Bingham similarly tried to expand the notion of the rule of law, increase the set of rights that were worthy of protection, and ensure that states respect international law focusing on the courts' ability to adjudicate rights.[254]

However, more minimalistic interpretations of the notion also gave paramount importance to courts. Raz's or Hayek's ideas on legal stability and foreseeability assume that courts will protect the legal expectations of individuals.[255] Finally, for those who value the procedural angle of the rule of law, the judiciary ensures that every individual is capable of vindicating their rights on the same footing both in terms of applicable law and of competent jurisdiction. For such theorists, the quintessence of the rule of law resides in the rationales that judges expound on in their decisions.[256] Alexandra Lahav has similarly argued that the judicial dimension is so central to the rule of law because "[e]ach person's case ought to be adjudicated based on the facts of that case and the applicable law, no matter who the litigant. This is the foundation of the rule of law."[257]

Such enthusiasm for judicial litigation is understandable. The judicial component is crucial to make sure that the law is clear and its effects are foreseeable, so that individuals can make plans and anticipate what would happen in a judicial controversy. Indeed, the intellectual movement that advocates simultaneously the globalization and judicialization of rights has reinforced this link between individualism, autonomy, and judicial protection of rights.[258] Kai Möller has identified a global model of constitutional rights that secures the vindication of individual claims under the prism of individual autonomy.[259] In

252 Dworkin, "Political Judges and the Rule of Law," 287.

253 Dworkin, 281. Similarly, Marcel Gauchet, *Le nouveau monde* (Paris: Gallimard, 2017) 577 ("[L]e motif de la popolarité de la justice dans une société d'individus: elle est ouverte, par nature, à des actions individuelles. Elle ne connait que des litiges particuliers.").

254 Thomas Henry Bingham, *The Rule of Law* (London: Penguin Books, 2011), 8.

255 Raz, *The Authority of Law*, 215–16; Hayek, *The Road to Serfdom*, 54.

256 Shklar, "Political Theory and The Rule of Law," 12.

257 Alexandra Lahav, *In Praise of Litigation* (New York: Oxford University Press, 2017), 115.

258 Anne Orford, "A Global Rule of Law," in *The Cambridge Companion to the Rule of Law*, ed. Jens Meierhenrich and Martin Loughlin (Cambridge: Cambridge University Press, 2021), 551.

259 Möller, *The Global Model of Constitutional Rights*, 74.

his words, "the constitution as a whole is best explained by a commitment to a comprehensive protection of personal autonomy."[260]

If courts have been considered the pinnacle of the rule of law, as they would epitomize the equal treatment of individuals, their capacity to make plans, and their protection from abuse, it is little or no surprise that, in the context of the constitution building processes in Afghanistan and Iraq, one of the first priorities among international human rights activists and organizations was improving the probabilities of "future litigation by local rights entrepreneurs," as the standard means of securing and promoting the values of constitutionalism.[261]

Within the individualist, rights-driven, and courts-driven approach of the rule of law, religious freedom claims do not always sit comfortably. Ran Hirschl has observed that there can be frictions between religion and the judicial protection of rights: although they are meant to protect rights, courts can actually exert a disruptive role on religious organizations and even the civil society at large. Hirschl notes that courts often take on a secularizing approach—a sort of "judicial antipathy" that emerges when faced with religious hierarchies or sources of law.[262] In Hirschl's view, courts "may loudly manifest their commitment to respecting tolerance, balancing rights, protecting the vulnerable, ensuring proportionality, and other important values," but "they may nevertheless interpret the situation as reflecting a more fundamental power struggle between competing systems of knowledge and interpretation: the earthly, human-enacted constitution and the claim to speak in a vernacular of a revealed or divine authority."[263]

2.2 *The Rule of Law and Religious Freedom*

Many aspects in the field of religious freedom have found uncontroversial support within contemporary legal culture and practice because they strongly resonate with the logic of the rule of law sketched above. The rule-of-law approach has distilled religious freedom as a right that should be vindicated in courts and granting a reasonably clear view of what is permitted or forbidden to religious and nonreligious believers.[264] As Dominic Avon has noted, this approach is centered on the individual, and resonates with the theories of great philosophers of Western modernity such as Rousseau, who defended freedom of conscience as a form of individual autonomy.[265] This understanding is still on dis-

260 Möller, 87–88.
261 Feldman, "Imposed Constitutionalism," 874.
262 Hirschl, *Constitutional Theocracy*, 203.
263 Hirschl, 204.
264 Avon, *La liberté de conscience*, 556.
265 Avon, 556.

play in constitutional theories that value freedom of religion as an asset in individualistic terms: it would provide individuals with a space in which they can make decisions about religion without suffering imposition from others.[266]

Within the framework of religious freedom, alongside the individual component lie the collective and institutional components. Religious activities usually take place in group and through institutions characterized by hierarchical structures, internal rules and means of jurisdictional redress. These collective and institutional features often frontally clash with the paradigms of modernity.[267] The return of traditional religions on the public scene in the last decades has inevitably made the status of religion and of religious communities more controversial within the framework of the rule of law.[268] If the natural dimension of the rule of law is the individual, religious freedom is increasingly an exception.[269]

Julian Rivers has argued that some friction between the state and the institutional component of religious freedom is inevitable: "[i]f religious associations are to have a role in the preservation of civil liberty, they must to some degree compete with the institutions of the [s]tate. They cannot be purely spiritual communities, in the ethereal sense of the word, but must be expressed in the material goods common to all humankind."[270] The worldly dimension of religions is precisely the aspect that often clashes with constitutional states, Hirschl notes, as "[w]hile accepting the mantra of diversity as inclusion, the high priests of constitutionalism appear to vehemently oppose the nonstate-law-as-competition narrative, at least in part because it challenges the very authority and superiority they hold on account of the secular order."[271]

Scholars such as Harold Berman have long argued that the competition between state and religious actors is healthy for democracies.[272] After all, as Victor Muñiz-Fraticelli observes, "freedom is guaranteed not only by the liberal principles internal or endogenous to the state, but also by the presence of external

266 Möller, *The Global Model of Constitutional Rights*, 67.

267 Antoine Compagnon, *Les antimodernes: de Joseph de Maistre à Roland Barthes* (Paris: Gallimard, 2016), 85.

268 Julian Rivers, *The Law of Organized Religions: Between Establishment and Secularism* (Oxford: Oxford University Press, 2010), 35.

269 Gauchet, *Le nouveau monde*, 146 (on the complex relationship between the political and the religious dimensions, and the Western difficulty in understanding religion in a non-individualistic fashion).

270 Rivers, *The Law of Organized Religions*, 336.

271 Hirschl, *Constitutional Theocracy*, 203.

272 Harold J. Berman, *Law and Revolution* (Cambridge, MA: Harvard University Press, 1983), 10.

authorities that push against state authority."[273] This positive outlook, however, has been increasingly questioned, and the paradigm of a healthy competition has been replaced by one that sees a pernicious fight being fought between state and religion. Such a fight inevitably prioritizes the state over religion, Ran Hirschl and Ayelet Schachar have argued, as "[i]n contemporary secularized nations, the role formerly granted to religion is conspicuously supplanted; a polity's constitutional framework is often its 'supreme law' and, as such, tends to infiltrate many facets of public and private life, just as religion has been traditionally wont to do."[274]

The conflict is of such a magnitude that Laborde has recently argued that religion per se cannot have a specific place in liberal societies. She has suggested erasing the notion of "religion" from the liberalism lexicon:[275] "Religion," in her words, "need not be singled out in the liberal state."[276] Since "[t]he liberal state does not uniquely protect *religious* beliefs and practices from intolerance, repression, and discrimination,"[277] religious freedom would be "only one instantiation of a more basic right—a right to personal freedom or ethical independence, which is also at stake in other controversies around war, conscience, sexuality, and abortion."[278]

The individualistic view of rights and the monodimensional, state-centric understanding of the legal order push the freedom of religious communities into the background; some even remove it from the pillars of liberal constitutions altogether. They tend to understand religious freedom in individualistic terms and often translate it into the more familiar notions of autonomy and self-determination while downplaying the importance of religious institutions and hardly acknowledging the existence of religious legal orders endowed with their own rules and judicial bodies.

The emphasis on the individual goes beyond state institutions and state constitutionalism. It has even become staple in religious narratives of religious freedom and interreligious dialogues, including the Muslim intellectual sphere[279]—although it has stopped short of suggesting that religious affilia-

---

273 Victor Manuel Muñiz Fraticelli, *The Structure of Pluralism: On the Authority of Associations* (Oxford: Oxford University Press, 2014), 246.

274 Ran Hirschl and Ayelet Shachar, "Competing Orders? The Challenge of Religion to Modern Constitutionalism," *University of Chicago Law Review* 85, no. 6 (2018): 432.

275 Laborde, *Liberalism's Religion*, 2.

276 Laborde, 13.

277 Laborde, 28.

278 Laborde, 28.

279 See especially "A Common Word Between Us and You," October 13, 2007, https://www.acommonword.com/the-acw-document/. The open letter was signed by 138 Muslim scholars and clerics. See also the Marrakesh Declaration on the Rights of Religious

tion and belonging should be deprioritized or mitigated to embrace a purely individualistic outlook.

After centuries of Ottoman practice of governance of and religious tolerance toward non-Muslim minorities,[280] religious freedom as a right is still contested in Islam[281] and modern legal texts on the subject are often considered ambiguous.[282] But significant statements such as "A Document on Human Fraternity for World Peace and Living Together," signed by Pope Francis and Grand Imam of Al-Azhar Ahmad al-Tayyeb, seem to endorse a fairly modern and Western understanding of religious freedom, which is centered on the individual and equal citizenship rather than the notions of minority and tolerance.[283] The document states that "each individual enjoys the freedom of belief, thought, expression and action," but also emphasizes the notion of "citizenship," which is "based on the equality of rights and duties, under which all enjoy justice." The document further argues that "[I]t is … crucial to stablish in our societies the concept of *full citizenship* and reject the discriminatory use of the term *minorities* which engenders feelings of isolation and inferiority … it undoes any successes and takes away the religious and civil rights of some citizens who are thus discriminated against." There is therefore also in the Muslim and Middle Eastern world a call to embrace an individual-based approach to religious freedom—one that deemphasizes the role of groups, rejects discriminations, and calls for a unified notion of citizenship that is fully applicable to all the citizens of a society.[284] Interreligious dialogues and religious freedom declara-

---

Minorities in Predominantly Muslim Majority Communities, Ministere des Habous et des affaires islamiques, January 27, 2016, https://habous.gov.ma/fr/rencontre-de-marrakech/3115-%E2%80%9Cthe-marrakech-declaration-on-the-rights-of-religious-minorities-in-the-muslim-world%E2%80%9D.html. The declaration was signed by some 300 Muslim scholars representing more than 120 countries.

280 Abdullah Saeed, *Islam and Religious Freedom: A Sourcebook of Scriptural, Theological, and Legal Texts*, ed. Matthew Anderson and Karen Taliaferro, The Religious Freedom Project, December 5, 2014, 49, https://berkleycenter.georgetown.edu/publications/islam-and-religious-freedom-a-sourcebook-of-scriptural-theological-and-legal-texts.

281 Saeed, *Islam and Religious Freedom*, 5.

282 Saeed, 5.

283 Pope Francis and Ahmad al-Tayyeb, "A Document on Human Fraternity for World Peace and Living Together," February 4, 2019, https://www.vatican.va/content/francesco/en/travels/2019/outside/documents/papa-francesco_20190204_documento-fratellanza-umana.html.

284 In a similar vein, a group of thirty-eight Islamic law scholars addressed Pope Benedict XVI for the statements he had made at the University of Regensburg on September 12, 2006, arguing against religious coercion by those who hold power. "Open Letter to His Holiness Pope Benedict XVI," accessed November 6, 2023, https://ammanmessage.com/media/openLetter/english.pdf.

tions promoted by religious groups seem to now look for a common ground between the extremes of individualism and the reality of political societies in the Middle East, which often operate according to a profoundly different logic, as I discuss briefly above in Part 1 and analyze in more detail below, in Part 3.

Despite the emphasis on the individual, also the West has slowly and partially come to terms with reality and acknowledged that some political and legal systems may enjoy stability *because* hierarchically ordered institutions beyond the state and often with clear religious affiliation mutually negotiate their place in the public sphere, not *despite* them. As I discuss in Part 3, this logic still pervades the Middle East. The constitutional model that has best absorbed this logic goes by the name of *consociation*.

2.3 *Western-Made Consociations: an Exception to the Norm?*

Liberal and communitarian thinkers have alternatively argued for an atomist or holistic understanding of political societies.[285] As Charles Taylor has explained, especially the English-speaking world has largely espoused a "family of theories of liberalism" that he calls "procedural:" within this framework, society is "an association of individuals, each of whom has his or her conception of a good or worthwhile life, and correspondingly, his or her life plan. The function of society ought to be to facilitate these life plans, as much as possible, and following some principle of equality."[286]

Taylor, along with other such prominent theorists as Hannah Arendt, Alasdair MacIntyre, Michael Sandel, Michael Walzer,[287] and Will Kymlicka,[288] has countered liberalism and heralded a wave of communitarian thinking, which has been especially successful in the late twentieth century. Such scholars have been fighting the atomistic view of human societies and its insistence on the individual. Their approach has often magnified the importance of groups and deemphasized the role of the individual, her pursuit of her own interest, and the centrality of procedures, but without challenging some of the key features of political liberalism encapsulated in the notion of the rule of law seen above.

As Taylor has made clear, communitarians do not overlook the benefits of a "common bulwark of our freedom and citizen dignity."[289] However, they

---

285 Charles Taylor, "Cross-Purposes: The Liberal-Communitarian Debate," in *Liberalism and the Moral Life*, ed. Nancy L. Rosenblum (Cambridge, MA: Harvard University Press, 1991), 159.

286 Taylor, "Cross-Purposes," 159.

287 George Kateb, "Democratic Individuality and the Meaning of Rights," in Rosenblum, *Liberalism and the Moral Life*, 182.

288 Kymlicka, *Liberalism, Community and Culture*, 165, 167.

289 Taylor, "Cross-Purposes," 171.

consider this approach insufficient rather than mistaken: political institutions should not just enable individuals to pursue their own life plans; they need to heed the call of democratic societies in search of "some commonly recognized definition of the good life."[290] Communitarians thus share with the supporters of liberalism the belief that people engage in social and political life through the democratic process to shape common policies, although they often disagree on whether such policies should be tailored to suit *only* individual life plans or *also* the common good. Only some of them, such as Kymlicka, who have heralded the notion of "multiculturalism" as an addition and not an alternative to individualistic liberalism, tend to believe that also "cultural membership" to subnational groups can be considered as a proper "good" worthy of protection.[291] In other words, the liberal/communitarian divide usually does not affect the widespread belief in the centrality of institutions that protect individuals.

Liberals and communitarians are both distant—although to a different degree—from scholars who have developed their theories around the notion of *belonging*. The notion of belonging, Dana Alexander has noted, challenges both "liberal ethos and discourse" and "a certain aspect of rights constitutionalism."[292] Alexander distills the idiosyncrasies between liberalism and belonging by noting that

> [t]he liberal rights ethic … is profoundly challenged by collective belonging. It is challenged by social and political belonging as a fundamental condition of human existence in tension with the Kantian concept of the universal, autonomous subject. It is challenged by the normative significance of given, pre-rational belonging and its associated values of mutual commitment and loyalty that are absent from the liberal moral scheme. It is challenged by the attribution of intrinsic value to the protection and preservation of a particular collective, irrespective of its value or utility to individual members.[293]

The notion of belonging goes beyond communitarianism because it greatly values the existence of "collective frameworks" in human societies. Collective frameworks "are structures—national or social—that grant people a sense of

290 Taylor, 160.
291 Kymlicka, *Liberalism, Community and Culture*, 165.
292 Dana Alexander, "Rights Constitutionalism and the Challenge of Belonging: An Empirical Inquiry into the Israeli Case," *Law & Social Inquiry* 1 (2022): 21.
293 Alexander, "Rights Constitutionalism and the Challenge of Belonging" 25.

belonging and security in face of various forces threatening the stability of their world."[294] Within the dimension of belonging, such frameworks are not simply of the same importance of individual rights; they often take priority over the individual, as Alexander adds: "when collective frameworks are perceived as insecure, the need to preserve them and fortify their boundaries is liable to take priority even for rights-espousing liberals, rendering the preeminence of human rights—on which liberal constitutionalism rests—difficult to justify in the sociopolitical sphere."[295]

Joseph David has offered a similar defense of the importance of belonging and of the institutions that give shape to it. In his view, the dimension of belonging is the backdrop against which the perception of sameness and otherness is built.[296] The impact of belonging on legal and political institutions is profound because it "enables our interpersonal relations, shapes our communal imaginations, and inspires in us feelings of solidarity."[297] Although belonging is important and even vital in generating and preserving collective identities, its dynamic between sameness and otherness must be handled with care, as it can easily trigger unfairness and social strife. In fact, "[o]therness is the result of a discursive process by which a dominant in-group (us, the self) constructs a dominated out-group (them, the other) by stigmatizing a real or imagined difference, which is presented as a negation of identity and thus a potential motive for discrimination."[298]

David concludes that the dynamic of belonging, with its categories of sameness and otherness, surfaces especially within deeply heterogeneous societies in which different groups are subject to different jurisdictions and make up different polities within the same body politic.[299] He thus paints a picture that largely depicts the Middle Eastern polities when he states that "[t]he tension between territorial jurisdiction, in which laws apply within a geographic area, and personal jurisdiction, in which laws apply to individuals based on their identity or belonging, was known in late ancient times. Broadly speaking, these two types of jurisdiction are not merely principles in the implementation of law, but also factors in the shaping of cultural and religious identity."[300]

---

294 Alexander, 22.

295 Alexander, 22.

296 Joseph E. David, *Kinship, Law, and Politics: An Anatomy of Belonging* (New York: Cambridge University Press, 2020), 9.

297 David, *Kinship, Law, and Politics*, 1.

298 David, 77.

299 David, 75.

300 David, 75.

The principles of the rule of law have primarily addressed "the fear of violence, the insecurity of arbitrary government and the discriminations of justice."[301] However, the axis around which the rule of law almost always rotates has become the individual. On the contrary, the rule of law seems to say little or nothing about the relationships *within* groups and the dynamics *among* them. Even communitarians have been largely preoccupied with the notion of the public good. A stronger interest in the inner dynamics of the groups that make up a body politic is visible among the intellectuals who have explored the dimension of belonging.

If theorists of belonging have challenged the notion of the rule of law on the theoretical plane, the reality and structure of political and legal communities that do not rotate around the axes of the individual, equal rights, and courts has surfaced through the notion of *consociations* during the second half of the twentieth century. Within the studies of consociations, the issues of belonging, loyalty, participation, and power dynamics have eventually taken central place. Lijphart's pioneering studies on consociations in the 1960s put the existence and functioning of political societies centered on identity groups that make reciprocal concessions and negotiate the national agenda in the academic and political spotlight.[302]

The notion of consociation has become particularly salient in contexts of peace-building, transitional justice, and political reconciliation.[303] In deeply divided societies that experienced internecine conflicts, the work of stopping violence, providing security and functioning institutions has meant coming to terms with the reality of local "social cleavages,"[304] for which consociationalism has become an important constitutional technique and a veritable asset.[305] Consociationalism protects the groups that make up the body politic, safeguards their autonomy, and ensures that they have a voice and a role in the decision-making processes, giving life to mechanisms of "power sharing."[306]

As Ori Avi-Guy has made clear, consociations do not aim to dilute group membership or mitigate groupthink to protect individuals and bring them closer to state institutions. On the contrary, they are "based on the assumption that internal gaps and hostility among rival groups are resistant to change and are at least semi-permanent, and therefore divisions over group identity

301 Shklar, "Political Theory and The Rule of Law," 16.
302 Arend Lijphart, "Consociational Democracy," *World Politics* 21, no. 2 (1969): 216–22.
303 Avi-Guy, "Transformation," 290.
304 Avi-Guy, 293.
305 Avi-Guy, 296.
306 Avi-Guy, 296.

cannot be bridged."[307] They accept the reality of the simultaneous existence within a body politic of different polities that have different values, laws, and sometimes even courts.

Such political structures are not mere relics of the past, exotic systems, or small and negligible ad hoc solutions of government that are unfamiliar to the West. Belgium's nineteenth century constitutional settlement is an example. In the Middle East, the first consociation slowly crystallized in the first half of the twentieth century, when the Lebanese state adopted a written constitution under French input in 1926.[308] Political negotiations in and between Lebanon and France culminated in the apportionment of parliamentary seats and other key political offices along religious lines.[309] More recent examples are traceable in different scenarios such as India, South Africa, Burundi, or Sudan.[310]

Consociations also played an important role in the late twentieth-century's Europe. In the 1990s, the conflicts in Bosnia-Herzegovina[311] and Northern Ireland[312] ceased after consociational compacts gave the fighting parties reciprocal veto-powers and required cross-group political majorities for bills of major political concern and impact. The United States was particularly involved in the Bosnia peace process that culminated in the Dayton Agreement of 1995,[313] which included the Constitution of Bosnia, giving birth to a power-sharing system. Bosnian citizens participated in the democratic process according to their religious and ethnic affiliation: Muslim Bosniaks, Catholic Croatians, and Orthodox Serbians.[314] Of smaller magnitude, but with several similarities with this consociationist model, are the constitutional settlements that the West brokered in other parts of the Balkan area.[315] To a different degree, all these

307 Avi-Guy, 299.

308 Edmond Rabbah, *La constitution libanaise: Origines, Textes et Commentaires* (Beirut: Publications de l'Université libanaise, 1982), 50.

309 Samuel Issacharoff, *Fragile Democracies: Contested Power in the Era of Constitutional Courts* (New York: Cambridge University Press, 2015), 7.

310 Horowitz, "Conciliatory Institutions and Constitutional Processes in Post-Conflict States," 1222.

311 Andrea Pin, "Il costituzionalismo consociativo. Libertà, sfera pubblica e partiti," *Percorsi costituzionali*, no. 1 (2019): 49.

312 Pin, "Il Costituzionalismo Consociativo," 49–50.

313 Ronald C. Slye, "The Dayton Peace Agreement: Constitutionalism and Ethnicity," *Yale Journal of International Law* 21, no. 2 (1996): 472.

314 United Nations, The General Framework Agreement for Peace in Bosnia and Herzegovina, Art. IV–V, December 14, 1995, https://peacemaker.un.org/bosniadaytonagreement95.

315 Florian Bieber, "Reconceptualizing the Study of Power-Sharing," *Südosteuropa* 60, no. 4 (2012): 527; Slaviša Orlović, "Consociational Experiment in the Western Balkans: Bosnia and Herzegovina and Macedonia," *New Balkan Politics*, no. 7 (2015), http://www.newbalkanpolitics.org.mk/item/consociational-experiments-in-the-western-balkans-bosnia-and-herzegovina-and-macedonia.

constitutional models arrange the apportionment of the public sphere along religious, language, or ethnic lines. By assigning everyone to a specific ethnic or religious faction and apportioning public posts accordingly, they make such groups indispensable mediators of political representation, deemphasizing the role of the individual and her autonomy in the political process. They make the dimension of belonging prevail over the individual self-determination.

The types of consociation vary significantly across a spectrum that comprises several different models, some of which are more distant than others from liberal societies governed by typically rule-of-law mechanisms. However, all these pacts have at least one feature in common:[316] they clash with one or more key aspects of the rule of law. They challenge individualism, rights narratives, and equality.

The values of individualism, rights, and equality were on full display when regime changes took place in Afghanistan and Iraq in the early twenty-first century. In these countries, global or Western coalitions that removed the national leadership and governed the transition during the drafting of new constitutional texts, trying to instill a culture centered on the rule of law. The ideals of Western constitutionalism were largely *the drivers* of the regime change. Therefore, recent constitutional developments in Afghanistan and Iraq were very different from those that occurred in Bosnia, Northern Ireland, or other parts of the world where Western forces and intellectuals encouraged consociational agreements to *end* internecine wars and high instability.

The net result of the constitutional efforts to instill a rule-of-law culture in Afghanistan and Iraq was probably negative: these two countries were badly run and had very low performances in terms of human rights protection with the Taliban and Saddam Hussein, but they suffered heightened levels of instability and collapsed afterward and probably because of the Western interventions and ideals. However, resorting to consociations was not a viable alternative.

Given the high regard in which the rule of law is kept in the West and around the world more generally, intervening in Afghanistan and Iraq and then rebuilding them through political and legal systems that did not fit with the notion of the rule of law was unrealistic: it would have been perceived as a failure, if not a betrayal of the international interventions that ousted the Taliban and Saddam Hussein. Contemporary constitutional culture seems so much focused on the rule of law and the individualistic logic that comes with it as indispensable requisites for the improvement of legal and political structures that a consociational compact was out of the question. Consociations that take into account religion, ethnicity, or other factors as politically and legally salient fac-

316 McGarry and O'Leary, "Iraq's Constitution of 2005," 675.

tors may be acceptable as ways to end bloodshed and civil wars, but they cannot be the goals of military and political efforts that inevitably cause victims, instability, and social unrest.

Unlike Afghanistan and Iraq, the Egyptian trajectory does not suggest that a consociational agreement would have given a post-Mubarak course a better chance to thrive. The Egyptian camp is not simply dominated by forces that conceive themselves as different political bodies, would like to divide the jurisdiction along religious lines, or adhere to the logic of groupthink. The conflict among Egyptian factions also lies on ideological grounds, which seem even harder to mitigate, as they cannot be countered with the power-sharing mechanisms that deal with localisms or ethnic or religious rivalries.[317] But Egypt still confirms the difficulty of entrenching the rule of law as a nonpartisan set of principles that can soothe everyone and on which everyone can easily or reasonably agree.

Conclusions

Although the West tried to end the political fragmentation and bloodshed more than once by resorting to consociationalism, it is not difficult to guess why it refused to do so in Afghanistan and Iraq, or why Egypt is unlikely to embrace it.

Afghanistan and Iraq were already destabilized and had a very disappointing level of respect for human rights prior to foreign interventions. But their new courses were a quintessentially or largely foreign product. International coalitions—within or outside the UN umbrella—effectively toppled the existing regimes with the aim of transforming those lands into states compliant with the rule of law. The international interventions in the Balkans or in the peace process that involved Ireland and the United Kingdom in Northern Ireland were considered viable solutions to end internecine wars; international coalitions assembled around the ideal of the rule of law could not suggest the same solution. Military and political interventions in Afghanistan and Iraq simply could not compromise and repudiate the basic ideas of autonomy, atomistic human rights, and equality.[318] Allowing the perpetuation of a variety of religious, ethnic, and tribal loyalties would have betrayed the prospect of replacing corrupt, human-rights violator regimes with rule-of-law-compliant democracies.

Squaring the reality of societies that are fragmented along sectarian lines with the requisites of the rule of law is not problematic just because these

317 Maboudi, *The "Fall" of the Arab Spring*, 220.

318 Franz Böhm, "Rule of Law in a Market Economy," in *Germany's Social Market Economy*, ed. Alan Peacock and Hans Willgerodt (London: Macmillan, 1989), 47.

attempts are made mainly from the outside. If the Afghani and Iraqi examples warn against rule-of-law inspired foreign interventions, the autochthonous Egyptian struggle for a democratic, rule-of-law compliant state tells a different story.

It is hardly questionable that Egypt has been ruled with the iron fist for decades and that recent years have just seen an increase in the role of the military. The constitution now in force permits military tribunals to handle cases of civilians,[319] statutes allow withdrawing citizenship in case of terrorism, and terrorism itself is so broadly defined that it covers multiple types of dissent.[320] The Muslim Brotherhood has also been removed from the public scene, in a move that, according to the regime, was intended to stabilize the fluid political dynamic, but has greatly impoverished the political outlook of Egypt.[321]

Many have rightly observed that law in Egypt has become a travesty that covers authoritarianism.[322] But there seems to be more than what meets the eye. Equating dissent with terrorism and withdrawing citizenship to those who challenge the military leadership are indicative of a deeply fragmented society.[323] Egyptian society is divided within the Muslim camp among those who support the military, those who put their hopes in the liberal model of constitutionalism, and those who believe in a democratically legitimized political Islam.

These three camps do not just disagree on their political agenda—they have widely different plans for the structure of the body politic. The military-run regime aims to stabilize the political spectrum and secure order; the Islamist faction supports a set of liberties that would be compatible with Islamic values and laws; the liberal camp has embraced a Western model of rights and guarantees.[324] Such a big ideological divide between Egyptian political factions is not ephemeral. It sits on a layer of religious sectarianism that has deep roots in Egyptian society and further weakens the prospects of a rule-of-law compliant state.

As seen in Part 1, religious jurisdictions, judges, and courts in Egypt were slowly—and not without difficulties—replaced with state laws, judges, and courts. The small period led by the Muslim Brotherhood saw the vigor of religious laws resurface. The al-Sisi regime has not prompted a sea change in the

319 Constitution of the Republic of Egypt, Art. 204; see Elgohari, "Deconstructing the Relation between Law and Authoritarianism," 464.
320 Elgohari, 468.
321 Al-Ali, *Arab Constitutionalism*, 48.
322 Elgohari, "Deconstructing the Relation between Law and Authoritarianism," 454.
323 Elgohari, 457, 462.
324 Al-Ali, *Arab Constitutionalism*, 50.

field, as it has granted some autonomy to religions. Thus, one of the main traits of continuity among different clusters of Egyptian society seems to consist of the priority in granting some degree of autonomy to religious communities and some variations in the legal status of individuals of different faiths.

As Azīz al-Azmeh has explained, Egypt has been constantly marked by an important role of religion in the political sphere. In the 1980s, once the Muslim Brotherhood was able to reorganize and fight against Anwar Sadat, a clash between religious factions ensued: "'Christian families' were formed as public organisations to confront 'Muslim families' in the universities, while in Upper Egypt ... [an] internecine confessional conflict [took place]."[325] Within the Muslim camp, "Suggestions were made using archaising Islamist language ... on the basis of the primacy ascribed to an Islamic political identity, and the subordinate, consociational satellitisation of Christians." "Such suggestions" replicated the consociational logic, as, they understood "citizens ... not so much [as] individual free persons but as members of groups defined by birth rather than by volition or formation. It implies the negation of secularism that guarantees the state the character of transcendence with respect to civic and private groups, and as the locus of a national political culture transcending collectivities of birth ... This discourse asserts the savagely identitarian definition of an individual."[326]

The consociational tone of the clashes that started in 1980s Egypt follows in the footsteps of Afghanistan and Iraq. It does not suggest that a consociational system would have worked better in Egypt than a liberal democracy, as the country is also deeply divided along ideological lines. But it confirms the deep-seated sectarian logic in the Middle East and further encourages a deeper appreciation of some common denominators of that political culture that do not easily fit the logic of the rule of law. The next Part focuses on the tradition upon which such a shared support for inequality, religious autonomy, and fragmentation of the body politic is based.

3 The Constitution of the Middle East and North Africa: the Arab Winter and the Failed Rule-of-Law Interventions

Introduction

Significant differences stand out between the recent constitutional developments in Afghanistan, Iraq, and Egypt. In Afghanistan, Western constitutional-

325 Azīz al-Aẓmeh, *Secularism in the Arab World: Contexts, Ideas and Consequences*, trans. David Bond (Edinburgh: Edinburgh University Press, 2021), 405.

326 Al-Aẓmeh, *Secularism in the Arab World*, 405–6.

ism retreated with foreign troops when the Taliban seized power again in 2021; the toppling of Saddam Hussein's regime left Iraq in a largely chaotic situation, where Iran seems to broker a fragile peace; and after years of turmoil, Egypt is subject to an iteration of its several autocratic regimes. However, despite the differences, these political and legal systems share some commonalities among themselves and with the broader Middle Eastern region.

For Al-Azmeh, such commonalities identify "a state, which in political science literature goes by the name of consociational." In the words of Al-Azmeh, in a consociational entity, the state

> [F]orms a vertical hinge of self-enclosed units, and, as in the case of the Lebanese state—and in the past fifteen years, extending to Iraq and Syria—forming a membrane for socio-political relations, without there being a stable network for such relations. In this arrangement, private institutions, often known as civil, share sovereignty with the state: these include local leaderships based on family and religious confession, and financial conglomerates with potentially armed complements sharing, with the state, the deployment for organised violence, and sharing with one another the oligarchic and patrimonial arrangement of public affairs. Within the subordinating state, confessionalism is based on the ideological and historiographic trope of continuity, presented by its adepts as an adequate explanation of a situation of great socio-historical complexity.[327]

Al-Azmeh recognized that the consociational "arrangement emerged in Lebanon from various historical contexts that divested capitalism of its capacities for abstraction, and also limited its possibilities of even a properly statist policy." However, in his opinion the Lebanese experiment "followed the template of the nineteenth-century European fantasy, the idea of a mosaic society, transposed to policy, coming to acquire reality in recent years"[328]—a mirage, as "recurring political and economic collapses would later confirm."[329]

Contrary to what Al-Azmeh argues, the sectarian apportionment of public posts was not the mere offspring of European imperialism and the Western-led process of decolonization. It actually resonated with the fabric of Middle Eastern political culture, as Michel Chiah, one of the leading figures of the Lebanese constitutional experiment, once noted, "[t]here are minorities here,

327 Al-Aẓmeh, *Secularism in the Arab World*, 404.

328 Al-Aẓmeh, 404–5.

329 Imad Salamey, "The Unmelting Lebanese National Pot," Canopy Forum, October 14, 2022, https://canopyforum.org/2022/10/14/the-unmelting-lebanese-national-pot/.

denominations there, and different cultures co-existing together everywhere. We should not argue for or against the particular rights of one or the other but rather simply recognize the rights of all ... Amicable coexistence ... would only be achieved through a political framework based on equal respect for the other's belief system and ... this would only be accomplished in an open assembly where each religious grouping and every region was represented as fully and as practically as possible."[330]

The disappointing outcome of the consociational structure established in the Lebanese constitution with European support does not disprove the deep roots of consociations in Middle Eastern societies. The Lebanese Constitution was just one of the earliest attempts to address the reality of political and constitutional fragmentation along religious and blood lines in the Middle East. In this Part I examine the categories along which the Middle Eastern political and constitutional culture has developed, showing how its structure and even its societal composition differs from those envisaged by rule-of-law theorists, starting with A. V. Dicey. Reflecting the overwhelming presence of Islam in the region, I make frequent references to this religious and intellectual tradition. Throughout the frequent turmoil that has characterized the modern Middle East, Islamic thinking has, in fact, provided a constant point of reference. It is particularly telling that after decades of forced secularism under Gamal al-Nasser, a weak Sadat presidency came to terms with a mounting Islamist wave, assigning in 1977 the prominent Al-Azhar Mosque in Cairo the task of drafting a project for an Islamic Constitution that would finally balance the rule of law with some Islamic principles.[331] Although the Al-Azhar project never materialized, copies of the Al-Azhar project were distributed in Tahrir Square during the revolution that ousted Mubarak in early 2011—thirty-four years, two presidents, and one revolution later.[332]

3.1 *Groups and Inequalities*

The provisions of the Constitutions of Afghanistan, Egypt, and Iraq discussed in Part 1 that enshrine basic values that stem from the notion of the rule of law are not exceptional in the Middle East. Most of the constitutional texts that appeared in the region have incorporated classic rule of law principles. They routinely emphasize the importance of equality among citizens, the respect

330 Michel Chiha, *Le Jour*, January 9, 1945, http://michelchiha.org/about-michel-chiha/political-career/political-philosophy/.

331 "Project for an Islamic Constitution," Distinguished Al-Azhar Academy for Islamic Research, 1977, Tahrir Documents, http://www.tahrirdocuments.org/wp-content/uploads/2011/07//مشروع-الدستور-الاسلامي.pdf.

332 The referential texts of the Arab Spring protests that took place in Tahrir Square in Cairo can be found at Tahrir Documents, http://www.tahrirdocuments.org.

for human beings irrespective of their gender, ethnic, or religious identity, and grant everyone access to justice.[333] The basic structure of such constitutional texts thus echoes the rule-of-law mentality that is typical of liberal systems, their emphasis on the issue of liberty and individualism, and their understanding of political institutions as pursuing common interests and courts hearing complaints and redressing injustices.[334] But such constitutional categories and mechanisms do not seem to reflect Middle Eastern societies adequately. Despite repeated efforts to Westernize them, such societies still seem to function according to significantly different rules.[335]

The first pillar of Middle Eastern societies is the group. In Middle Eastern societies, the individual is immersed in ethnic and religious structures that perform political functions.[336] This applies to both the Islamic community—the *ummah*—and the rest of religious and ethnic groups, which in the Koran are named with the same word.[337] At least since the time of the great medieval Islamic thinker Ibn Khaldun,[338] the dominant religious community in the Middle East has constantly seen itself and other religions and ethnicities as groups within which individuals and families find their primary political identity and affiliation, enjoy their rights, and are expected to discharge their obligations.[339] Their approach is reflected in the Islamic law notion of *millah*, which identifies a section of the polity with a specific set of rights and duties and gave birth to the Ottoman *millet* system, in which an individual's religious affiliation controlled his or her personal status and social, economic, and institutional relations.[340]

---

333 Constitution of the Republic of Afghanistan 2004, Preamble; Constitution of the Republic of Iraq 2005, Preamble.

334 Esmaeili, "The Nature and Development of Law in Islam and the Rule of Law Challenge in the Middle East and the Muslim World," 338–39.

335 Brown, *The Rule of Law in the Arab World*, 29–30.

336 Emile Tyan, *Institutions du Droit Public Musulman* (Beirut: CEDROMA, 1999), 111.

337 Tyan, *Institutions du Droit Public Musulman*, 107.

338 Mohammed Talbi, "Ibn Ḫaldūn et le sense de l'histoire," *Studia Islamica*, no. 26 (1967): 74, 89.

339 Muḥammad Khātamī, *La religion et la pensée prises au piège de l'autocratie: Voyage au cœur de la pensée politique des musulmans pendant l'essor et au déclin de la civilisation islamique* (Leuven: Peeters, 2005), 303–4.

340 Paul S. Rowe, "Neo-millet Systems and Transnational Religious Movements: The *Humayun* Decrees and Church Construction in Egypt," *Journal of Church and State* 49, no. 2 (2007): 331; see also Suraiya Faroqhi, "The Ottoman Ruling Group and the Religions of Its Subjects in the Early Modern Age: A Survey of Current Research," *Journal of Early Modern History* 14, no. 3 (2010): 239 ("[T]he Ottoman ruling group assumed that Jews, as well as Christians of various denominations, had their places, inferior but well established, within the society of the Empire.").

This approach is not unique to Islam. In the same vein, Christian denominations in the Middle East often understand and identify themselves as subnational entities of the national polity: state laws allow them to enjoy specific sets of rights and duties, address family issues according to their religious laws and solve disputes in their religious courts.[341] This practice reflects and reinforces a legal mentality that is not centered on the individual and his or her legal claims, but rather the group to which he or she belongs.[342]

The political and legal significance of the individual in the stereotypical rule-of-law scenario diverges significantly from the Middle Eastern situation. In the latter case, individuals are first and foremost members of their ethnic or religious group. It is primarily through their membership to a certain group that they are recognized as members of the society at large.[343] The national polity thus sits on a layer of different groups whose primary goal consists in self-preservation[344] and that mutually recognize each other and negotiate the polity's common goals.[345]

Membership in a certain group is not just—and not even primarily—a matter of personal preference. As Avishai Margalit and Joseph Raz have pointed out, membership requires "mutual recognition:" "one belongs" to a certain group "if, among other conditions, one is recognized by other members of the group as belonging to it."[346] This type of recognition *within* a group generates a sense of protection against other groups: the individual is protected *because* he or she is a member of a certainly socially and publicly recognized faction. Middle Eastern societies thus provide their members with some level of invulnerability not through their state institutions, as rule of law-based societies do, but through their belonging to a certain faction.[347] In other words, where the

341 Fiona McCallum, "Christians in the Middle East: A New Subfield?," *International Journal of Middle East Studies* 42, no. 3 (2010): 487.

342 Kristina Stoeckl, *The Russian Orthodox Church and Human Rights* (London: Routledge, 2014), 8 ("[I]t is … difficult to 'derive' liberal individual human rights from Orthodox theology.").

343 Pin, *Il* rule of law *come problema*, 145.

344 Lawrence Rosen, "Islamic Conceptions of the Rule of Law," in Meierhenrich and Loughlin, *The Cambridge Companion to the Rule of Law*, 89 ("To most Islamic legal thinkers the preservation of a community of believers (*umma*) free from social chaos (*fitna*) is a foremost consideration and toward that end the founders of the four main schools of Islamic law were quite prepared to defer to political authority.").

345 Pin, *Il* rule of law *come problema*, 145–46.

346 Avishai Margalit and Joseph Raz, "National Self-Determination," *Journal of Philosophy* 87, no. 9 (1990): 445.

347 Michael Walzer, *Spheres of Justice: A Defense of Pluralism and Equality* (New York: Basic Books, 2010), 31 (on the role of the state in protecting its citizens).

rule of law recognizes each individual as a member of the polity and endowed with a certain set of rights,[348] in the prevailing Middle Eastern culture the individuals are recognized as members of the polity through the recognition of their group.

As seen above, the segmentation of the political and legal sphere in different religious camps is especially visible in Iraq, which hosts a great deal of religious diversity. Sunnis, Shias, and several Christian denominations have inhabited its territories for centuries, sharing the same space and interacting with each other, but still living according to different laws. Analogies also abound in Afghanistan, which has been dominated by a mix of ethnic, religious, and tribal affiliations. The composition of Afghani society is a complex web of loyalties, which often interact and intermingle, but nevertheless identify each individual as a member of one—or multiple—groups. The 2004 constitution of Afghanistan recognized some of these social institutions when it acknowledged the jurisdiction of religious courts, but other institutions and mechanisms have also operated in an informal fashion.[349] Paradoxically, the limited recognition of religious laws in Afghanistan, without any significant sectarian apportionment of public posts, has excessively simplified the scenario, underestimating the political salience of religious, ethnic, and tribal rules, and therefore undercutting the legitimacy of the constitution itself.

Despite the significant presence of Copts, Egypt's social component and institutional composition are marked by a much less diversified variety of groups, but analogies with Iraq and Afghanistan are not lacking. Although it was enacted after the purge of the Muslim Brotherhood, also the latest constitutional text, that of 2014, subjects Muslims, Christians, and Jews to different laws, thereby according to them differing sets of rights and duties.[350] Such sets of rights and obligations are not the product of the will of these groups of believers: they are predetermined by the community they belong to. Individuals are thus qualified by their membership to a certain community and by the laws that are applicable to them.

An additional layer of complexity resides in the ideological spectrums, as Egyptians have constantly disagreed on the consociational or liberal option for their Constitution. The predominantly Sunni camp is divided into those who advocate a fully fledged constitutional state, the military protection, or

---

348 Walzer, *Spheres of Justice*, 252–53.

349 Lutforahman Saeed, *Islam, Custom and Human Rights: A Legal and Empirical Study of Criminal Cases in Afghanistan after the 2004 Constitution* (Cham: Springer, 2022), 5.

350 Constitution of the Republic of Egypt 2014, Art. 3 ("The principles of the laws of Egyptian Christians and Jews are the main source of laws regulating their personal status, religious affairs, and selection of spiritual leaders.").

the resurrection of Islamic law.[351] Within the political camp there is less ideological stability—as conservatives can become liberal and vice versa—but still a strong political and legal rivalry. No faction has truly committed to giving up its political success to generate a pluralistic environment, within which several worldviews can peacefully coexist. Militarism still represses civil society—and increasingly so after al-Sisi took power.[352] The Muslim Brotherhood adheres to a logic that is still keen to divide the public sphere into religiously homogeneous factions that would be dominated by Islamic law priorities.

The groupmind logic that permeates Middle Eastern societies does not just divide the public sphere into factions and subjects them to different rules and institutions. It also often makes them particularly stable and even resilient. In a society that operates along religious, ethnic, or tribal lines, as is particularly the case of Afghanistan and Iraq, individuals are discouraged from leaving their group or even just distancing themselves from it. Groups are institutions that provide their members with relationships, protection, and mechanisms of redress in which citizens tend to be locked.[353]

Institutionalization of religious groups and groupmind logic exert special pressure on decisions related to religious freedom. Instead of being a matter for individuals to decide, acts and processes of conversion are powerful political acts that relocate the individual within another group or even outside the institutional and legal mechanisms that govern a polity. This happens not just within Islam, some of whose variants often discourage or prohibit conversion,[354] but also within other religious factions that do not simply lose a member when somebody converts but also suffer an erosion of their demographic and political importance. Freedom to convert is widely considered a critical aspect of freedom of conscience or even a litmus test to assess the quality of the protection of freedom of conscience within a legal system. But in the Middle East conversions can be powerful—and even dangerous—political acts of rebellion against a certain institutional and legal system.[355] In this respect, Middle Eastern societies seem to encourage social and religious stability also as a means to secure political stability, and vice versa: political mobilization can in fact destabilize the relationships among the ethnic or religious factions.

---

351 Jamal and Kensicki, "A Theory of Critical Junctures for Democratization," 203.

352 Elgohari, "Deconstructing the Relation between Law and Authoritarianism," 461.

353 Pin, *Il* rule of law *come problema*, 175–77.

354 Anderson and Talia, "Development of Religious Freedom in Islamic Thought," 9–11.

355 Avon, *La liberté de conscience* 1077–78.

3.2 *Equality among Groups and Public Institutions*

In the Middle East, equality is perceived as a matter of power dynamics among competing groups, rather than as a quality of the relationships among individuals and between individuals and public powers. The Islamic differentiation between the rights and duties of men and women is just part of a broader scenario, within which groups are given a specific role and are protected as such. Groups pursue comparable or equal degrees of safety to preserve their ability to self-govern and self-assert with other groups.

Although the legal status of groups in Egypt has greatly modernized, Egyptian Muslims and Christians still remain within the orbit of their respective legal regimes. The Afghan society is still fragmented in a variety of ethnic and religious loyalties that pervade social, economic, and political relations. To some extent, Afghans are *equally* members of tribal and religious networks that identify them, make them part of specific polities, and entrust them with identifiable rights and duties. The unstable political environment in Iraq and the influence on Iran on its domestic affairs reflect the sense of vulnerability—even danger—that many groups perceive under the 2005 constitution and their lack of domestic cross-sectarian cohesion.

Equality in the Middle East therefore has a distinct meaning that overlaps only partially and intermittently with the mentality that characterizes regimes that adhere to the traditional understanding of the rule of law. Instead of putting individuals on an equal footing, the Middle Eastern political culture focuses on the mutual protection—and even self-preservation—of groups. Perfect equality may not be achieved, since for Islamic law the Muslim community discharges a specific role of protector of the rest of society;[356] but the focus is still on the collective dimension, and it is the balance among the collectivities that is of primary concern for the preservation of social and political equilibrium. To achieve such equality among collectivities, groups tend to be cohesive and to exert considerable pressure on their members to remain within their rankings.

This logic reflects itself in the institutional mechanisms that operate in such societies. State institutions in the Middle East do not primarily govern the state polity, but rather ensure that each smaller polity thrives and operates according to its own rules. This approach has deep roots in the culture of the region and has a special point of reference in the Medina Pact—or "Constitution of Medina"—that the Prophet Muhammad signed with the Jewish minorities of his new city and the literature that followed afterwards;[357] but the importance

---

356 Emon, "Reflections on the 'Constitution of Medina,'" 107–9, 120.

357 On the constitutional nature of the pact and its authenticity, see Emon, 'Reflections on the 'Constitution of Medina,'" 107–9, 120.

of constitutional settlements as mutual insurances among religions and groups can also be found in the most recent Afghan, Egyptian, or Iraqi constitutional trajectories and in their failures. The constitutions that were drafted under sizable foreign input in Afghanistan and Iraq did not acknowledge or reflect the complexity of the national social mosaics. The Afghan 2004 failed to consider ethnic groups and tribes, and even forbade tribe-based parties, thereby both undermining its legitimacy and alienating local groups that the Taliban were quick to recruit. In Iraq, a ban on Baʿathists prevented prominent Sunni figures from participating in the new political course and alienated vast portions of the Sunni population. In itself, the apportionment of seats among religious groups Iraq did not disappoint Iraqis; it simply failed to assuage minorities because the majority groups have hijacked it, as they have been able to take political control of many of those seats to aggrandize their presence in Parliament: the Shia majority has thus seized power through the democratic mechanisms, instigating the Sunnis to fight the new constitution rather than participating in the institutional life after Saddam.[358] Through the constitutional texts that frenetically replaced each other, Egypt pursued dramatically alternative constitutional and political agendas, thereby making the life of representative institutions impossible.

The role of judicial redress in the Middle East also differs considerably from the ideal of the rule of law. From an empirical perspective, the most visible difference between the Middle East and the rule-of-law paradigm is probably the existence of multiple religious courts that deal with matters of importance for citizens and adjudicate them on the basis of their religion.[359] The unity of jurisdiction that Dicey probably overemphasized when he celebrated the English system vis-à-vis the French judiciary is very distant from this logic and reality.[360] When parties vindicate their *religious* rights in *religious* courts do not channel their claims through state institutions—they call on their religious community to address their case; the state will simply acknowledge and give effect to such decisions. The state serves as an enforcer of religious laws as applied in religious courts, thereby abdicating the legislative and judicial powers implied by the notion of the rule of law.

A second, profound difference between legal systems centered on the rule of law and Middle Eastern courts resides in the notion of justice, redress, and in the role of the judiciary at large. By pitting individuals or groups against each other, judicial disputes can endanger the membership of an individual to a cer-

358 Aid to the Church in Need, "Iraq."

359 Womack, "Christian Communities in the Contemporary Middle East," 189, 194.

360 Dicey, *Introduction to the Study of the Law of the Constitution*, 115.

tain group or the political equilibrium that religious and ethnic communities usually manage to preserve through negotiations and mutual concessions.[361] In the Middle Eastern mosaic of memberships and loyalties, individual judicial claims may be perceived as eroding the connecting tissue among the members of a certain group or the social glue among groups.[362] It is not surprising that Islam has constantly devolved a contentious issue to an arbitrator, who "at once intercedes (even usurps) the power of the state to decide issues but does so in such a way as to reinforce local conventions and customary practices."[363] The nonjudicial way of solving disputes has played a prominent role in preserving cohesion within and among groups.

The importance of respecting conventions and customs is such a key to ensure that individuals and groups enjoy social acceptance in the Middle East, that a recent empirical study on the judicial system and practice in Afghanistan has acknowledged that "[m]ost Afghans consider society as a judge and believe that they must have society's approval concerning their personal and social lives. They usually think that they must have the acceptance of the community in terms of their behavior and daily activities, even when it comes to their personal issues ... It would be very difficult to go against the norms that society has established for its members in Afghanistan."[364]

Mediation and arbitration are not the ideal for a of redress in Afghanistan just because the judicial system envisioned by the 2004 constitution has failed.[365] Such conciliatory, informal ways of redress are the offspring of the robust web of loyalties and local customs. In Afghanistan, the opinion of ordinary people who have no legal education or training but are still respected in the local community and know local customs affect judicial decisions: courts are keen to consider them also in cases that would be controlled by Shariʿa or other legal provisions.[366] The custom-based approach, in turn, reinforces the holistic approach to justice, as custom routinely reflects the societal notion of the good in a certain circumstance.[367]

361 Pin, *Il* rule of law *come problema*, 145–46.
362 Pin, 177.
363 Rosen, "Islamic Conceptions of the Rule of Law," 96.
364 Saeed, *Islam, Custom and Human Rights*, 36.
365 Saeed, 38.
366 Saeed, 34.
367 Saeed, 34.

In the same vein, and despite growing discontent,[368] in Egypt premodern forms of dispute resolution are still in use.[369] They address and resolve even violent religious clashes, such as the church bombings that occurred in the country in the late 2010s.[370] The preferred method of handling such events has consisted in customary process of informal reconciliation or mediation, which have replaced formal investigations with hearings that often comprise members of the Al-Azhar University and the Coptic Church.[371] Such processes rarely identify those responsible for violent attacks, as they primarily try to soften tensions and to restore a certain degree of social cohesion among religious groups.[372]

Deeply divided societies avoid entrusting courts with the capacity to "tame religious-based conflicts and intercommunal tensions."[373] Negotiations between groups seem to be preferred because among their core concern is the respect of the mosaic of groups that make up the national polity.[374] The negotiation dynamics replicates and reinforces the logic that puts groups rather than individuals at the center.

3.3 *Reframing Religious Freedom for the Middle East: Rediscovering Consociations*

A reappreciation of the Middle East, its social fabric, and the political and constitutional culture that has dominated it for centuries encourages a fresh look at the most realistic possibilities to secure religious freedom and stability in the region.

In the Middle East, religious freedom is not an individual affair, nor is it a social fact that has nothing to do with state institutions. Religions exert a political role that goes far beyond the moral and ethical teachings that may guide believers at the ballot box. Religions, along with tribes and other ethnic entities and affiliations, are indispensable components of national political institutions. Institutional mechanisms, such as arbitrators, that have emerged over the centuries to develop, enact, and enforce laws reflect the mediative role of religions and ethnic groups. Excluding such groups and their power of negotiation from the political sphere often threatens political institutions.

---

368 Aid to the Church in Need, "Egypt," in *Religious Freedom Report 2023*, https://acninternational.org/religiousfreedomreport/reports/country/2023/egypt.

369 "2022 Report on International Religious Freedom: Egypt."

370 "Christianity in the Middle East," 4.

371 "Christianity in the Middle East," 9.

372 "Christianity in the Middle East," 4.

373 Hirschl and Shachar, "Competing Orders?," 439.

374 Margalit and Raz, "National Self-Determination," 447.

The preservation of ethnic and religious groups and of peaceful relations among them also has a profound impact on social mobility and religious freedom. In fact, the stability of political life usually requires internal cohesion within each group. Strong bonds often discourage individual mobility between groups and religious conversions that would alter the demographic equilibrium among groups. If freedom of conversion is high on the checklist of religious freedom, its limited availability often serves as a political stabilizer in the Middle East.

Promoting the rule of law as a recipe for fundamental rights and religious freedom can backfire in the Middle East because the fundamentals of the rule of law can jeopardize traditional links between religious groups, religious stability, and political stability. Individualism, individual equality, and the importance of judicial redress are key factors in the rule of law that can hardly be smoothly implanted in the region. A more moderate and realist approach, one that takes advantage of rather than replaces existing religious and social institutions, is probably more productive. Proponents of the rule of law in the West and in the Middle East should realize that their expectations may thwart the processes of constitution building and even trigger sectarian hostilities in the region.

The dynamics of power and the rapid regime changes that occurred in Egypt show that its political culture is not divided along ethnic and religious lines only. Al-Sisi, the Muslim Brotherhood, and many supporters of liberal constitutionalism all belong or are at least formally affiliated with the Islamic camp. Divisions exist within the Coptic camp, as some of its members have grown skeptical of the strong personal and professional ties that link Coptic pope Tawandros and al-Sisi and have advocated rights for Copts through a secular approach, leveraging the electoral process rather than through the special relations between their religious leaders.[375] However, the power struggles in Egypt show that the rule of law has not become a common denominator capable of hosting all political factions. The promoters of constitutional liberalism, the Muslim Brotherhood, and the military that have supported al-Sisi—all thought that the constitution should reflect their own political and legal agenda. Whereas the proponents of constitutional liberalism never seized power, the Muslim Brotherhood and the military that replaced them were both capable of transposing their ideas into constitutional texts. The conflicts between the prioritization of Islamic law, of the Ummah, and of religious groups in the case of the Muslim Brothers, and of the centrality of the

375 "Christianity in the Middle East," 9; Womack, "Christian Communities in the Contemporary Middle East."

military and of the presidency after the demise of Mohammad Morsi's regime, testify to the fact that the liberal ideals encapsulated in the rule of law did not provide a common ground for Egyptian society: They were contentious ideals, which important players in Egypt did not embrace.

Significant portions of Middle Eastern societies have not put their bets on the rule of law. They still conceive themselves as parts of a multireligious political mosaic, within which they perceive to be more protected, especially if they are demographically minoritarian.

Conclusions

A bird's eye view of the trajectory of some Middle Eastern countries suggests that expecting rule-of-law-centered constitutions to replace dictatorships with decent democracies that are committed to the judicial protection of rights and to equality among citizens often underestimates important aspects of the Middle Eastern constitutional culture. Such aspects cannot and should not be treated as merely vicious practices in need of replacement with fully fledged rule-of-law principles and rules. Even more fundamentally, it is naïve to believe that it would be sufficient to remove Middle Eastern autocrats or religious fanatics to let dynamic and vibrant constitutional settings centered on the rule of law flourish. Some practices reflect deeply rooted political cultures and should not be disposed of too easily.

Sectarian apportionments of political institutions and the customs of negotiating mutual concessions among factions are important practices of peoples who find themselves more attached to their religious, tribal, or ethnic authorities than to their national authorities. Replacing such systems with rule-of-law constitutional principles and institutions that do not compromise on their individualistic logic, the legal and political irrelevance of tribal, religious, or ethnic ties, and the unavailability of mechanisms of negotiations, reconciliation, and redress beyond the state may not heal religious wounds and end persecutions in territories that endured autocracy or religious totalitarianism. As it has been noted about Afghanistan and Iraq, securing democratic elections and institutions may be feasible; but it is just the beginning, and it is probably much easier than securing the functioning of a decent rule of law system.[376] Good intentions notwithstanding, such initiatives may worsen or trigger social clashes that traditional political structures may be better equipped to keep under check.

The failed attempts to instill the rule-of-law logic in the Middle East stem from a misunderstanding of the region and the underestimation of what the

376 Fukuyama, "Why Is Democracy Performing So Poorly?," 14.

rule of law requires. Some constitutional and legal systems may simply operate under different premises than those that embrace the rule of law and resist dramatic or gradual transplant that spans decades and aims to instill a culture that complies with the standard requirements of the rule of law.

The best example of the resilience of such political cultures is probably Lebanon. Its constitutional text is the oldest in force of the Middle East, as it was enacted in 1926. Lebanon was not intended to be a permanently consociational system that would operate according to a sectarian allocation of public posts. In fact, section H of the Preamble to the constitution states that "[e]liminating political sectarianism is a basic national objective, to be achieved according to a transitional plan."[377] However, the sectarian apportionment of parliamentary seats along religious lines has never been questioned and is still considered a factor of moderation for the troubled small state of the Levant.[378] Its sectarian constitutional settlement is further reinforced by the customary distribution of apex government roles, which has constantly awarded Catholic Maronites with the presidency of the republic, Sunnis with the presidency of the Council of Ministries, and Shia with the presidency of the parliament. This arrangement is so steeped in the Lebanese political system that when the Civil War tilted the balance in favor of Sunnis, the constitution was amended to give more powers to the leader of the executive power and their representative, instead of reshuffling the apex roles among the three main communities considering the power shifts.[379]

Unsurprisingly, sectarian systems do not easily morph into rule of law regimes where individualism, equality among individuals, political representation, and courts replace groups, sectarian apportionment of institutional roles, religious courts, and nonjudicial negotiations. Sectarian societies often prize social stability, discourage trans-group mobility and individualism, and favor groupthink. There seems to be therefore very little political or personal incentive to leave such institutions behind.[380] Consociational systems may not be the optimal option, but they are hardly just transitional.

George Kateb took a very hard stance against the legal recognition of collective identities when he argued that legal systems that define one's identity

---

377 Constitution of Lebanon 1926, Preamble.

378 Salamey, "The Unmelting Lebanese National Pot."

379 Andrea Pin, "La Gracile Costituzione del Libano," *Quaderni Costituzionali* 28, no. 1 (2008): 171.

380 Francesco Palermo and Lorenzo Somigli, "The 'Scramble for Lebanon': Is Federalism a Way out of the Deadlock of Consociationalism?," International Institute for Middle East and Balkan Studies, April 15, 2023, https://www.ifimes.org/en/researches/the-scramble-for-lebanon-is-federalism-a-way-out-from-the-deadlock-of-consociationalism/5158?#.

based on his or her culture are antithetical to the respect for human dignity. In his words, cultural identity "[may] be imagined as one's fated and irrevocable personal identity. Affiliation that is self-defining and life-defining with this intensity gives a person a hand-me-down identity, an identity that has completion and enclosure, which no personal identity that is free of self-mystification can possibly have. One's life becomes a vicarious experience, lived through the fate of the group. Group rights consign individuals to dependence sustained by their conformity."[381]

Although pitting collective and individual identity against each other is controversial, Kateb probably has a point in suggesting that such systems prevent people from making choices individually and from moving freely within their own polity; but he omits that it is often *through* their cultural identity that they gain recognition, protection, and even freedom. Entrenching the rule of law in such systems without jeopardizing the enjoyment and protection of religious freedom may prove to be almost a Sisyphean task, as religious freedom—or at least the type of religious freedom the system is capable of granting—*is* often protected *through* the system itself that the rule of law would like to dismantle.

People's identity may be in flux, and the stability that ethnically and religiously diverse societies achieve through difficult intergroup agreements can slow down the speed of the change or even deter it. But trying to uproot those agreements and dismantle those ethnic and religious institutions to replace them with constitutional settings that revolve around individual choice and mobility can have pernicious effects on the political and social system at large. Such attempts can make them instable or even chaotic, endangering the equilibrium among groups and the lives of those who live within them. Religious freedom and the rule of law may not flourish or perish simultaneously. Sometimes, there is a trade-off between them.

Concluding Remarks

In 2003, while the constitutions of Afghanistan and Iraq were coming to life, the Grand Chamber of the European Court of Human Rights delivered a unanimous judgment that exemplifies the gap between the expectations that the rule of law encapsulates and the Middle Eastern political and legal fabric.

381 George Kateb, *Human Dignity* (Cambridge, MA: Belknap Press of Harvard University Press, 2011), 11–12.

Refah Partisi v. Turkey ruled on the decision of the Turkish Constitutional Court to shut down the Islamist party Refah and confiscate its goods.[382] The party challenged the Constitutional Court decision, arguing that its ruling violated Article 10 of the European Convention on Human Rights, which protects the freedom of association. Such a drastic decision of the Turkish court was not unprecedented, since it had already removed political parties from the domestic public sphere, when it found that they threatened the constitutional principle of secularism. This time, the Turkish court shut down the party because, during an electoral campaign, some of its representatives argued in favor of reestablishing the Ottoman principle of personal jurisdiction and reinstating Islamic law as part of the law of the land. The European Court found that the Turkish Constitutional Court ruling did not violate the European Convention and ruled in favor of Turkey.

The Grand Chamber argued that the eventual restoration of Islamic law would have caused such a great damage to the rights enshrined in the European Convention on Human Rights that the dissolution of the party was justified. It explained that "a plurality of legal systems, as proposed by Refah, cannot be considered to be compatible with the Convention system."[383] It further added that "[Shariʿa] is incompatible with the fundamental principles of democracy."[384] In fact, the court reasoned,

> Refah's policy was to apply some of [Shariʿa]'s private-law rules to a large part of the population in Turkey (namely Muslims), within the framework of a plurality of legal systems. Such a policy goes beyond the freedom of individuals to observe the precepts of their religion, for example by organising religious wedding ceremonies before or after a civil marriage (a common practice in Turkey) and according religious marriage the effect of a civil marriage … This Refah policy falls outside the private sphere to which Turkish law confines religion and suffers from the same contradictions with the Convention system as the introduction of [Shariʿa].[385]

382 *Refah Partisi et al. v. Turkey*, apps. 41340/98, 41342/98, 41343/98 and 41344/98, 13 February 2003.

383 *Refah Partisi et al. v. Turkey*, apps. 41340/98, 41342/98, 41343/98 and 41344/98, 13 February 2003, Par. 119.

384 *Refah Partisi et al. v. Turkey*, apps. 41340/98, 41342/98, 41343/98 and 41344/98, 13 February 2003, Par. 123.

385 *Refah Partisi et al. v. Turkey*, apps. 41340/98, 41342/98, 41343/98 and 41344/98, 13 February 2003, Par. 127.

The Grand Chamber reiterated the judgment of first instance given by the Third Section of the Court, which ruled in favor of Turkey, stating that "[Shariʿa], which faithfully reflects the dogmas and divine rules laid down by religion, is stable and invariable. Principles such as pluralism in the political sphere or the constant evolution of public freedoms have no place in it."[386]

What the European Court of Human Rights found incompatible with the Convention are crucial aspects of political and constitutional systems in the Middle East. Stable legal regimes that recognize groups before individuals and accord to each group different rights, duties, and courts are the hallmarks of the legal and political orders that have developed in the region for centuries.

Key international and regional players seem to have made the same mistake when they conceived or promoted new constitutional compacts in the Middle East. They promoted them in a counterproductive way, as they instigated the development of legal orders based on the basic premises of the rule of law. They took for granted that a sound constitution-building process should focus on individual autonomy, national self-government, and rights.[387] They did not realize that they were stepping into a realm that was characterized by the cultural and political domination of groups, religious or ethnic-based rules, and reciprocal duties of loyalty.

The rule-of-law logic they proposed was not just alien to the political and religious institutions of the region; it was perceived as an attack on the mindset that permeates them. Replacing groupthink with individualism, tribal and communitarian negotiations with individual claims and tribunals centered on rights, and compromises with political competition threatened the political role of religion, ethnicity, and tribe.

Regarding religious freedom, the expectations that the rule of law would bring about more liberty for believers and churches were fraught with the mistaken belief that religion in the Middle East plays the same role that it retains in the West. When talking about the Middle East, Brett Scharffs has rightly pointed out that that "promoting religious freedom contributes to stability and security in post-conflict and peacebuilding settings of strategic significance;" but the type of religious freedom that the Middle East is familiar with has a stronger political and institutional component than in the West.[388]

386 *Refah Partisi et al. v. Turkey*, apps. 41340/98, 41342/98, 41343/98 and 41344/98, 13 February 2003, Par. 123 (citing par. 72 of the judgment of first instance).

387 Roberto Gargarella, *The Law as a Conversation among Equals* (Cambridge: Cambridge University Press, 2022), 29–30.

388 Brett G. Scharffs, "A Commitment to Religious Freedom as the Bond that Makes Us Free: Reinvigorating Security, Religious Autonomy, and the Good Society," *Review of Faith & International Affairs* 20, no. 4 (2022): 22.

The mistakes that characterized the foreign interventions in Afghanistan and Iraq doomed the constitutional changes they triggered. However, Afghanistan and Iraq may have the potential to stabilize and become more peaceful if they find an equilibrium among the groups that have often fought each other, rather than if they dismantle them. Paradoxically, the Egyptian scenario is ethnically and religiously less diverse than Afghanistan and Iraq, but it appears to be even more complicated. The triangular relationship between the Muslim Brotherhood, the supporters of the rule of law, and the military and its leaders see the constitution very differently. Fractions of Muslims and Christians disagree with their co-religionaries on how to handle religious identity and diversity. A grip on liberties, a fully fledged rule-of-law constitutional state, and a consociational compact that would integrate the Christian minority into a majoritarian Muslim society that applies Islamic law are alternative constitutional agendas, around any of which Egyptian society has not been able to coalesce. It would be, and has been, a mistake, however, to measure political and constitutional development with liberal constitutionalism and its appreciation of individual rights, equality, and litigation in courts. Egyptian intellectuals, political parties, and groups disagree on what many take for granted: that the rule of law would be a perfect common currency for the political and legal scenario.

Hirschl and Shachar have stated that "[t]he rule of law and the rule of God appear to be on a collision course," as they would be an "odd couple of sorts, diametrically opposed in many respects."[389] The trajectory of Afghanistan, Egypt, and Iraq confirms their belief and even suggests that rule-of-law narratives conceal some hubris. The rule of law as established in Afghanistan and Iraq had the presumption of replacing religion as a strong institutional, legal, and political asset. This may resonate with the Western trajectory of secularization of social, political, and legal institutions, but seems distant from the cultural makeup of the Middle East.

The distance between the rule-of-law logic and Middle Eastern dynamics is hardly just a product of the overwhelming presence and culture of Islamic religion. It seems more of a widespread logic that cuts across places and cultures. Protecting religious freedom *within* a rule-of-law system that does not compromise on its individualistic, state-centered logic, in the Middle East can prejudice *both* religious freedom and the stability of political and legal systems.

The legal and political systems of the Middle East have accorded religious freedom, protection, and political agency to religious groups through a complex web of loyalties and belongings that the prevailing notions of the rule of

389 Hirschl and Shachar, "Competing Orders?," 425.

law underestimate or do not understand. This region can best heal its wounds, achieve some stability, and provide people with religious freedom by compromising on key aspects of the rule of law, incorporating groupthink and group membership, and finding ways to establish them in their constitutional settings, rather than fighting them. This approach may mean encouraging rather than fighting tribal and religious parties and sectarian apportionment; fostering power-sharing solutions; and even social stability rather than mobility.

If my diagnosis is correct, there is reason to believe that the recommendation of Thomas Berg on the polarization of the debates on religious freedom in the United States is also applicable in the Middle East: "the morality of social-political conflict" requires "that we rightly press for justice but must also exercise humility as we do so."[390] Religious freedom concerns in the Middle East should not be inextricably linked with concerns about the rule of law and constitutionalism at large. These notions very often require a lot from peoples and states: individualism, liberalism, rights, and courts. Expecting that entire regions of the world espouse such thick notions as a precondition for them to enjoy the benefits of other quintessential goods, such as religious freedom, is simply too much and too simplistic. The extra-constitutional settlements that have surfaced in the Middle East, softening the individualistic, nonsectarian logic of the rule of law, are worthy of more consideration than they usually receive. They are the ways in which many peoples of the region have reconciled their centuries-old ways of living with the rule of law, thereby displaying a dose of pragmatism that several theories and practices based on the notion of the rule of law seem to have resisted or even opposed.

Bibliography

"2022 Report on International Religious Freedom: Afghanistan." US Department of State, Office of International Religious Freedom. https://www.state.gov/reports/2022-report-on-international-religious-freedom/afghanistan/.

"2022 Report on International Religious Freedom: Egypt." US Department of State, Office of International Religious Freedom. https://www.state.gov/reports/2022-report-on-international-religious-freedom/egypt/.

"2022 Report on International Religious Freedom: Iraq." US Department of State, Office of International Religious Freedom. https://www.state.gov/reports/2022-report-on-international-religious-freedom/iraq.

390 Thomas C. Berg, *Religious Liberty in a Polarized Age* (Grand Rapids: Eerdmans, 2023), 334.

Abdi, Kamyar. "From Pan-Arabism to Saddam Hussein's Cult of Personality." *Journal of Social Archeology* 8, no. 1 (2008): 3–36.

Ackerman, Bruce. *Revolutionary Constitutions: Charismatic Leadership and the Rule of Law*. Cambridge, MA: Belknap Press of Harvard University Press, 2019.

Agreement for Bringing Peace to Afghanistan between the Islamic Emirate of Afghanistan Which Is not Recognized by the United States as a State and Is Known as the Taliban and the United States of America, February 29, 2020. https://perma.cc/3PZ5-YRJJ.

Ahmed, Faiz. *Afghanistan Rising: Islamic Law and Statecraft between the Ottoman and British Empires*. Cambridge, MA: Harvard University Press, 2017.

Aid to the Church in Need. "Afghanistan." In *Religious Freedom Report 2023*. https://acninternational.org/religiousfreedomreport/reports/country/2023/Afghanistan.

Aid to the Church in Need. "Egypt." In *Religious Freedom Report 2023*. https://acninternational.org/religiousfreedomreport/reports/country/2023/egypt.

Aid to the Church in Need. "Iraq." In *Religious Freedom Report 2023*. https://acninternational.org/religiousfreedomreport/reports/country/2023/iraq.

Alexander, Dana. "Rights Constitutionalism and the Challenge of Belonging: An Empirical Inquiry into the Israeli Case." *Law & Social Inquiry* 1 (2022): 1–34.

Ali, Zaid al-. *Arab Constitutionalism: The Coming Revolution*. Cambridge: Cambridge University Press, 2021.

Aloosy, Massab al-. "With Iraq's Quota System the New Government is More of the Same." Arab Gulf States Institute in Washington, November 15, 2022. https://agsiw.org/with-iraqs-quota-system-the-new-government-is-more-of-the-same/.

Arato, Andrew. *Constitution Making under Occupation: The Politics of Imposed Revolution in Iraq*. New York: Columbia University Press, 2009.

Arjomand, Said Amir. "Constitutional Developments in Afghanistan: A Comparative and Historical Perspective." *Drake Law Review* 53, no. 4 (2005): 943–62.

Aswani, ʿAla al-. *La dittatura: racconto di una sindrome*. Translated by Giancarlo Carlotti. Milan: Feltrinelli, 2020.

Avi-Guy, Or. "Transformation—Overcoming the Limits of Liberal Peace and Transitional Justice in Deeply Divided Societies: Reconciliation in Liberal Peace Theory." *Israel Law Review* 54, no. 3 (2021): 289–304.

Avon, Dominique. *La liberté de conscience: histoire d'une notion et d'un droit*. Rennes: Presses universitaires de Rennes, 2020.

Ayoub, Samy A. "A Theory of a State? How Civil Law Ended Legal Pluralism in Egypt." *Journal of Law and Religion* 37, no. 1 (2022): 133–52.

Aẓmeh, Azīz al-. *Secularism in the Arab World: Contexts, Ideas and Consequences*. Edinburgh: Edinburgh University Press, 2021.

Barber, N. W. *The Constitutional State*. Oxford: Oxford University Press, 2010.

Barber, N. W. *The Principles of Constitutionalism*. Oxford: Oxford University Press, 2018.

Barfield, Thomas. "Afghanistan's Ethnic Puzzle: Decentralizing Power Before the U.S. Withdrawal." *Foreign Affairs* 90, no. 5 (2011): 54–58, 59–62, 63–65.

Beatty, David M. *Faith, Force, and Reason: An Armchair History of the Rule of Law.* Toronto: University of Toronto Press, 2022.

Berg, Thomas C. *Religious Liberty in a Polarized Age*. Grand Rapids: Eerdmans, 2023.

Berman, Harold J. *Law and Revolution*. Cambridge, MA: Harvard University Press, 1983.

Bieber, Florian. "Reconceptualizing the Study of Power-Sharing." *Südosteuropa* 60, no. 4 (2012): 526–35.

Bingham, Thomas Henry. *The Rule of Law*. London: Penguin Books, 2011.

Blackwill, Robert D. "Plan B in Afghanistan: Why a De Facto Partition is the Least Bad Option." *Foreign Affairs* 90, no. 1 (2011): 42–50.

Böhm, Franz. "Rule of Law in a Market Economy." In *Germany's Social Market Economy*, edited by Alan Peacock and Hans Willgerodt, 46–67. London: Macmillan, 1989.

Brown, Nathan J. *The Rule of Law in the Arab World: Courts in Egypt and the Gulf.* Cambridge: Cambridge University Press, 1997.

"Cardinal Louis Sako Returns to Baghdad," Iraqi News, April 14, 2024. https://www.iraqinews.com/iraq/cardinal-louis-sako-returns-to-baghdad/.

Carter, Joe. "5 Facts About Persecution of Christians in the Middle East and North Africa." Ethics & Religious Liberty Commission, May 31, 2019. https://erlc.com/resource/5-facts-about-persecution-of-christians-in-the-middle-east-and-north-africa/.

Chiha, Michel. *Le Jour*, January 9, 1945. http://michelchiha.org/about-michel-chiha/political-career/political-philosophy/.

Chilton, Adam S., and Mila Versteeg. *How Constitutional Rights Matter*. New York: Oxford University Press, 2020.

Choudhry, Sujit. "Old Imperial Dilemmas and the New Nation-Building: Constitutive Constitutional Politics in Multinational Polities." *Connecticut Law Review* 37, no. 4 (2005): 933–45.

"Christianity in the Middle East: Report 1." Christianity in the Middle East, 2021. http://www.christianitymiddleeast.gr/publications/reports/367-christianity-in-the-middle-east-cme-report-no-1.

Colley, Linda. *The Gun, the Ship, and the Pen: Warfare, Constitutions, and the Making of the Modern World.* New York: Liveright, 2021.

Compagnon, Antoine. *Les antimodernes: de Joseph de Maistre à Roland Barthes*. Paris: Gallimard, 2016.

"Confrontation in the Gulf: Transcript of President's Address to Joint Session of the Congress." *New York Times*, September 12, 1990, A20. https://www.nytimes.com/1990/09/12/us/confrontation-gulf-transcript-president-s-address-joint-session-congress.html.

David, Joseph E. *Kinship, Law, and Politics: An Anatomy of Belonging*. New York: Cambridge University Press, 2020.

Dawisha, Adeed. *The Second Arab Awakening: Revolution, Democracy, and the Islamist Challenge from Tunis to Damascus*. New York: Norton, 2013.

Devlin, Patrick. *The Enforcement of Morals*. Oxford: Oxford University Press, 1965.

Dicey, A. V. *Introduction to the Study of the Law of the Constitution*. 8th ed. London: MacMillan, 1915.

Dixon, Rosalind. *Responsive Judicial Review: Democracy and Dysfunction in the Modern Age*. New York: Oxford University Press, 2022.

Dodge, Toby. "Iraq and Muhasasa Ta'ifia: The External Imposition of Sectarian Politics." Foreign Policy Centre, November 12, 2018. https://fpc.org.uk/iraq-and-muhasasa-taifia-the-external-imposition-of-sectarian-politics/.

Dodge, Toby. "Muhasasa Ta'ifiya and Its Others: Domination and Contestation in Iraq's Political Field." In *Religion, Violence, and the State in Iraq*, Project on Middle East Political Science, 38–46. Crown Center for Middle East Studies, Brandeis University, October 2019. https://pomeps.org/muhasasa-taifiya-and-its-others-domination-and-contestation-in-iraqs-political-field.

Dworkin, Ronald. "Political Judges and the Rule of Law." Maccabean Lecture in Jurisprudence, 13 December 1977. *Proceedings of the British Academy*, no. 64 (1978): 259–87.

Ekins, Richard. "The State and Its People." *American Journal of Jurisprudence* 66, no. 1 (2021): 49–67.

Ekins, Richard, and Jeffrey Goldsworthy. "The Reality and Indispensability of Legislative Intentions." *Sydney Law Review* 36, no. 1 (2014): 39–68.

Elgohari, Mohamed. "Deconstructing the Relation between Law and Authoritarianism: How Law Consolidated Authoritarianism in Post-2011 Egypt." *Arab Law Quarterly* 36, nos. 4–5 (2022): 452–75.

Esmaeili, Hossein. "The Nature and Development of Law in Islam and the Rule of Law Challenge in the Middle East and the Muslim World." *Connecticut Journal of International Law* 26, no. 2 (2011): 329–66.

Fadel, Mohammad. "Al-Qadi." In *The Oxford Handbook of Islamic Law*, edited by Anver M. Emon and Rumee Ahmed, 301–27. Oxford: Oxford University Press, 2018.

Faroqhi, Suraiya. "The Ottoman Ruling Group and the Religions of Its Subjects in the Early Modern Age: A Survey of Current Research." *Journal of Early Modern History* 14, no. 3 (2010): 239–66.

Fearon, James D. "Iraq's Civil War." *Foreign Affairs* 86, no. 2 (2007): 2–15.

Feldman, Noah. "Imposed Constitutionalism." *Connecticut Law Review* 37, no. 5 (2005): 857–89.

Feldman, Noah. *What We Owe Iraq: War and the Ethics of Nation Building*. Princeton: Princeton University Press, 2006.

Fraticelli, Victor Manuel Muñiz. *The Structure of Pluralism: On the Authority of Associations*. Oxford: Oxford University Press, 2014.

Fukuyama, Francis. *Political Order and Political Decay: From the Industrial Revolution to the Globalization of Democracy*. New York: Farrar, Straus and Giroux, 2015.

Fukuyama, Francis. "Why Is Democracy Performing So Poorly?" In *Democracy in Decline?*, edited by Larry Diamond and Marc F. Plattner, 11–24. Baltimore: John Hopkins University Press, 2015.

Gardner, Frank. "Iraq's Christians 'Close to Extinction,'" BBC, May 23, 2019. https://www.bbc.com/news/world-middle-east-48333923.

Gargarella, Roberto. *The Law as a Conversation among Equals*. Cambridge: Cambridge University Press, 2022.

Gauchet, Marcel. *Le nouveau monde*. Paris: Gallimard, 2017.

Ginsburg, Tom, and Aziz Huq. "What Can Constitutions Do? The Afghan Case." *Journal of Democracy* 25, no. 1 (2014): 116–30.

Giorgio, Michele, and Alaa al Aswany. "Young People Will be the Leaders of the new Egyptian Revolution," Near East News Agency, April 8, 2017. https://nena-news.it/alaa-al-aswany-young-people-will-be-the-leaders-of-the-new-egyptian-revolution/.

Grimm, Dieter. "Levels of the Rules of Law on the Possibility of Exporting a Western Achievement." *European-Asian Journal of Law and Governance* 1, no. 1 (2011): 5–12.

Haber, Romy. "Fostering a Security Architecture for Minorities in the Levant: Failed Shots." *IACL-AIDC Blog*, October 20, 2022. https://blog-iacl-aidc.org/lebanon/2022/10/20/fostering-a-security-architecture-for-minorities-in-the-levant-failed-shots.

Habermas, Jürgen. "Constitutional Democracy: A Paradoxical Union of Contradictory Principles?" *Political Theory* 29, no. 6 (2001): 766–81.

Habermas, Jürgen. *Morale, diritto, politica*. Edited by Leonardo Ceppa. Turin: Einaudi, 2007.

Habermas, Jürgen. "Notes on a Post-secular Society." *New Perspectives Quarterly* 25, no. 4 (2008): 17–29.

Habermas, Jürgen. "Reflections and Hypotheses on a Further Structural Transformation of the Political Public Sphere." *Theory, Culture & Society* 39, no. 4 (2022): 145–71.

Haddad, Fanar. "Shia-centric State Building and Sunni Rejection in Post-2003 Iraq." Carnegie Endowment for International Peace, January 7, 2016. https://carnegieendowment.org/2016/01/07/shia-centric-state-building-and-sunni-rejection-in-post-2003-iraq-pub-62408.

Haider, Huma. "The Persecution of Christians in the Middle East." Institute of Development Studies, K4D Report 042, February 16, 2017. https://www.ids.ac.uk/publications/the-persecution-of-christians-in-the-middle-east/.

Hartogs, Jessica. "ISIS Cuts Fighters' Salaries Due to 'Exceptional Circumstances.'" CNBC, January 20, 2016. https://www.cnbc.com/2016/01/20/isis-cuts-fighters-salaries-due-to-exceptional-circumstances.html.

Hasim, Ahmed. "Saddam Husayn and Civil-Military Relations in Iraq: The Quest for Legitimacy and Power." *Middle East Journal* 57, no. 1 (2003): 9–41.

Hayek, Friedrich A. *The Road to Serfdom*. London: Routledge, 1962.

Helfont, Samuel. *Compulsion in Religion: Saddam Hussein, Islam, and the Roots of Insurgencies in Iraq*. New York: Oxford University Press, 2018.

Hill, Enid. "Al-Sanhuri and Islamic Law: The Place and Significance of Islamic Law in the Life and Work of 'Abd al-Razzaq Ahmad al-Sanhuri, Egyptian Jurist and Scholar, 1895–1971 [Part II]." *Arab Law Quarterly* 3, no. 2 (1988): 182–218.

Hirschl, Ran. *Constitutional Theocracy*. Cambridge, MA: Harvard University Press, 2010.

Hirschl, Ran, and Ayelet Shachar. "Competing Orders? The Challenge of Religion to Modern Constitutionalism." *University of Chicago Law Review* 85, no. 6 (2018): 425–55.

Hogg, Peter W., and Cara F. Zwibel. "The Rule of Law in the Supreme Court of Canada." *University of Toronto Law Review* 55, no. 3 (2005): 715–32.

Horowitz, Donald R. "Conciliatory Institutions and Constitutional Processes in Post-conflict States." *William & Mary Law Review* 49, no. 4 (2008): 1213–48.

Hourani, Albert. *Storia dei popoli arabi*. Milan: Mondadori, 1991.

Hunter, Erica C. D. "Persecution of Christians by Isis Contradicts Idea of a Caliphate." The Conversation, July 28, 2014. https://theconversation.com/persecution-of-christians-by-isis-contradicts-idea-of-a-caliphate-29710.

Hutt, Donald Bello. "Rule of Law and Political Representation." *Hague Journal of the Rule of Law*, no. 14 (2021): 1–25.

Ignatieff, Michael. *Empire Lite: Nation-Building in Bosnia, Kosovo and Afghanistan*. London: Vintage, 2003.

Ignatieff, Michael, and Amy Gutmann. *Human Rights as Politics and Idolatry*. Princeton: Princeton University Press, 2003.

"Iraq: The Isolation of Cardinal Sako," Information and Analysis on the Life of the Church, February 4, 2024. https://fsspx.news/en/news/iraq-isolation-cardinal-sako-42239.

Issacharoff, Samuel. *Fragile Democracies: Contested Power in the Era of Constitutional Courts*. New York: Cambridge University Press, 2015.

Jamal, Amal, and Anna Kensicki. "A Theory of Critical Junctures for Democratization: A Comparative Examination of Constitution-Making in Egypt and Tunisia." *Law and Ethics of Human Rights* 10, no. 1 (2021): 185–222.

Johnson, Constance A. *Iraq: Legal History and Traditions*. Washington, DC: Law Library of Congress, 2004.

Johnson, Daniel. "What Iraq Can Learn from De-Nazification." *Wall Street Journal*, April 22, 2013. https://www.wsj.com/articles/SB105095981621579000.

Kant, Immanuel. *Groundwork of the Metaphysics of Morals*. Edited and translated by Mary Gregor and Jens Timmermann. Cambridge: Cambridge University Press, 2012.

Kateb, George. "Democratic Individuality and the Meaning of Rights." In *Liberalism and the Moral Life*, edited by Nancy L. Rosenblum, 183–206. Cambridge, MA: Harvard University Press, 1991.

Kateb, George. *Human Dignity*. Cambridge, MA: Belknap Press of Harvard University Press, 2011.

Keane, Conor. US *Nation Building in Afghanistan*. London: Routledge, 2017.

Khaitan, Tarunabh. *A Theory of Discrimination Law*. Oxford: Oxford University Press, 2015.

Khātamī. Muhammad. *La religion et la pensée prises au piège de l'autocratie: Voyage au cœur de la pensée politique des musulmans pendant l'essor et au déclin de la civilisation islamique*. Leuven: Peeters, 2005.

Kuru, Ahmet T. *Islam, Authoritarianism, and Underdevelopment: A Global and Historical Comparison*. New York: Cambridge University Press, 2019.

Kymlicka, Will. *Liberalism, Community and Culture*. Oxford: Clarendon Press, 1992.

Kymlicka, Will. "Devolution and the Promotion (or Evasion) of Minority Rights." In *Federalism and Decentralization in the Contemporary Middle East and North Africa*, edited by Asli Ümmühan Bali and Omar Dajani, 50–66. Cambridge: Cambridge University Press, 2022.

Laborde, Cécile. *Liberalism's Religion*. Cambridge, MA: Harvard University Press, 2017.

Lahav, Alexandra. *In Praise of Litigation*. New York: Oxford University Press, 2017.

Laws, John. *The Constitutional Balance*. Oxford: Hart, 2020.

Lijphart, Arend. "Consociational Democracy." *World Politics* 21, no. 2 (1969): 207–25.

Lijphart, Arend. *Patterns of Democracy: Government Forms and Performance in Thirty-Six Countries*. 2nd ed. New Haven: Yale University Press, 2012.

Lombardi, Clark B. and Shamshad Pasarlay. "Constitution-Making for Divided Societies: Afghanistan." In *Constitutionalism in Context*, edited by David S. Law, 89–112. Cambridge: Cambridge University Press, 2021.

Maboudi, Tofigh. *The "Fall" of the Arab Spring: Democracy's Challenges and Efforts to Reconstitute the Middle East*. Cambridge: Cambridge University Press, 2022.

Margalit, Avishai, and Joseph Raz. "National Self-Determination." *Journal of Philosophy* 87, no. 9 (1990): 439–61.

Marrakesh Declaration on the Rights of Religious Minorities in Predominantly Muslim Majority Communities, January 27, 2016. https://habous.gov.ma/fr/rencontre-de-marrakech/3115-%E2%80%9Cthe-marrakech-declaration-on-the-rights-of-religious-minorities-in-the-muslim-world%E2%80%9D.html.

Mawlawi, Ali al-. "Salvaging State Legitimacy in Iraq through Decentralization." In *Federalism and Decentralization in the Contemporary Middle East and North Africa*, edited by Asli Ümmühan Bali and Omar Dajani, 120–39. Cambridge: Cambridge University Press, 2022.

May, Larry. “Bystanders, the Rule of Law, and Criminal Trials.” *Nomos*, no. 50 (2011): 241–64.

McCallum, Fiona. “Christians in the Middle East: A New Subfield?” *International Journal of Middle East Studies* 42, no. 3 (2010): 486–88.

McCrudden, Christopher, and Brendan O’Leary. *Courts and Consociations: Human Rights versus Power-Sharing*. Oxford: Oxford University Press, 2013.

McDougall, Walter A. *The Tragedy of* U.S. *Foreign Policy: How America’s Civil Religion Betrayed the National Interest*. New Haven: Yale University Press, 2016.

McGarry, John, and Brendan O’Leary. “Iraq’s Constitution of 2005: Liberal Consociation as Political Prescription.” *International Journal of Constitutional Law* 5, no. 4 (2007): 670–98.

Melcangi, Alessia, and Paolo Maggiolini. “Christians Navigating through Middle East Turbulences: The Case of the Copts in Egypt.” In *Migrants and Religion: Paths, Issues, and Lenses*, edited by Laura Zanfrini, 175–204. Leiden: Brill, 2020.

Melcangi, Alessia, and Riccardo Redaelli. “The Re-sectarization of the Middle East: Minorities, Communities and Identity Politics within the Current Geopolitical Confrontation.” In *Protection of Cultural and Religious Minorities*, edited by Ida Caracciolo and Umberto Montuoro (Turin: Giappichelli, 2019), 117–36.

Merdzanovic, Adis, and Kalypso Nicolaidis. “Advocacy for a Citizen-Centric Rule of Law Agenda: How Do We Bring the Rule of Law to Life?” *European Law Journal* 27, nos. 1–3 (2021): 297–305.

Miller, Richard W. “Might Still Distorts Right: Perils of the Rule of Law Project.” In *Nomos: Getting to the Rule of Law*, edited by James E. Fleming, 265–92. New York: New York University Press, 2011.

Möller, Kai. “Two Conceptions of Positive Liberty: Towards an Autonomy-Based Theory of Constitutional Rights.” *Oxford Journal of Legal Studies* 29, no. 4 (2009): 757–86.

Morr, Awad el-. “The Supreme Constitutional Court of Egypt and the Protection of Human and Political Rights.” In *Islam and Public Law: Classical and Contemporary Studies*, edited by Chibli Mallat, 229–60. London: Graham and Trotman, 1993.

Mounstephen, Philip. “Bishop of Truro’s Independent Review for the Foreign Secretary of FCO Support for Persecuted Christians: Final Report and Recommendations.” British Asian Christian Association, 2019. https://www.britishasianchristians.org/baca-news/bishop-of-truros-independent-review-for-the-foreign-secretary-of-fco-support-for-persecuted-christians-final-report-and-recommendations/.

Munadi M. Sultan. “Afghan Case Against Christian Convert Falters,” *New York Times*, March 26, 2006. https://www.nytimes.com/2006/03/26/international/asia/afghan-case-against-christian-convert-falters.html.

Nabeel, Gilgamesh, and Saad Salloum. “Christians in Post-2003 Iraq: Fragmentation Dynamics, Ethnic and Sectarian Fault Lines.” Centre Français de Recherche sur l’Irak,

August 11, 2023. https://cfri-irak.com/en/article/christians-in-post-2003-iraq-fragmentation-dynamics-ethnic-and-sectarian-fault-lines-2023-08-11.

Norton, Augustus Richard. "Al-Najaf: Its Resurgence as a Religious and University Center." *Middle East Policy* 18, no. 1 (2011): 132–45.

Oehring, Otmar. *Christians and Yazidis in Iraq: Current Situation and Prospects*. Sankt Augustin: Konrad-Adenauer-Stiftung, 2017.

O'Mahony, Anthony. "Christianity in Modern Iraq." *International Journal for the Study of the Christian Church* 4, no. 1 (2004): 121–42.

"Open Letter to His Holiness Pope Benedict XVI." https://ammanmessage.com/media/openLetter/english.pdf.

Orford, Ann. "A Global Rule of Law." In *The Cambridge Companion to the Rule of Law*, edited by Jens Meierhenrich and Martin Loughlin, 538–66. Cambridge: Cambridge University Press, 2021.

Orlović, Slaviša. "Consociational Experiment in the Western Balkans: Bosnia and Herzegovina and Macedonia." *New Balkan Politics*, no. 7 (2015). http://www.newbalkanpolitics.org.mk/item/consociational-experiments-in-the-western-balkans-bosnia-and-herzegovina-and-macedonia.

Palermo, Francesco, and Lorenzo Somigli. "The 'Scramble for Lebanon': Is Federalism a Way out of the Deadlock of Consociationalism?" International Institute for Middle East and Balkan Studies, April 15, 2023. https://www.ifimes.org/en/researches/the-scramble-for-lebanon-is-federalism-a-way-out-from-the-deadlock-of-consociationalism/5158?#.

Papa, Massimo. *Afghanistan: tradizione giuridica e ricostruzione dell'ordinamento tra Šarīʿa, consuetudini e diritto statale*. Turin: Giappichelli, 2006.

Pasarlay, Shamshad. "The Myth of a Constitution's 'Goodness': What We Get Wrong about Afghanistan's 1964 Constitution." *International Journal of Constitutional Law Blog*, January 26, 2022. https://www.iconnectblog.com/the-myth-of-a-constitutions-goodness-what-we-get-wrong-about-afghanistans-1964-constitution/.

Patterson, Eric. "How Did We Get Here? Religious Freedom Never Took Off in Afghanistan." *Cornerstone Forum* (blog), August 27, 2021. https://religiousfreedominstitute.org/how-did-we-get-here-religious-freedom-never-took-off-in-afghanistan/.

Pfiffner, James P. "US Blunders in Iraq: De-Baathification and Disbanding the Army." *Intelligence and National Security* 25, no. 1 (2010): 76–85.

Pin, Andrea. "A Constitution with Two Faces," Fondazione Oasis, March 1, 2007. https://www.oasiscenter.eu/en/a-constitution-with-two-faces.

Pin, Andrea. "La Gracile Costituzione del Libano." *Quaderni Costituzionali* 28, no. 1 (2008): 171–94.

Pin, Andrea. "Il costituzionalismo consociativo. Libertà, sfera pubblica e partiti." *Percorsi costituzionali*, no. 1 (2019): 45–60.

Pin, Andrea. *Il* rule of law *come problema: le sfide dell'Europa centro-orientale, della Brexit e del Medio Oriente*. Naples: Edizioni scientifiche, 2021.

Pin, Andrea. "Religious Persecution and Constitution Building in the Middle East: The Rule-of-Law Conundrum." *Notre Dame Law Review Reflection* 97, no. 3 (2022): 245–63.

"President Ends Recognition of Chaldean Patriarch, Putting Christian Assets at Risk," Asia News, December 7, 2023. https://www.asianews.it/news-en/President-ends-recognition-of-Chaldean-patriarch,-putting-Christian-assets-at-risk-58782.html.

Přibáň, Jiří. "Imaginary of the Rule of Law and a Force of Societal Transition: Central and East European Lessons from European (Dis)integration." In *Rule of Law in Crisis: Constitutionalism in a State of Flux*, edited by Martin Belov, 67–86. Abingdon: Routledge, 2023.

Pope Francis and Ahmad al-Tayyeb. "A Document on Human Fraternity for World Peace and Living Together." February 4, 2019. https://www.vatican.va/content/francesco/en/travels/2019/outside/documents/papa-francesco_20190204_documento-fratellanza-umana.html.

"Project for an Islamic Constitution." Distinguished Al-Azhar Academy for Islamic Research, 1977. Tahrir Documents. http://www.tahrirdocuments.org/wp-content/uploads/2011/07//مشروع-الدستور-الاسلامي.pdf.

Rabbah, Edmond. *La constitution libanaise: Origines, Textes et Commentaires*. Beirut: Publications de l'Université libanaise, 1982.

Rashwan, Eman. "The Price of Transitional Justice: A Cost-Benefit Analysis of Its Mechanisms in Post-revolution Phase." *University of Bologna Law Review* 6, no. 1 (2021): 95–142.

Rasul, Azhi. "Chaldean Patriarch Leaves Baghdad for Kurdistan." Rudan, July 15, 2023. https://www.rudaw.net/english/middleeast/iraq/150720231.

Rawls, John. *The Law of Peoples*. Cambridge, MA: Harvard University Press, 1999.

Raz, Joseph. *The Authority of Law*. Oxford: Clarendon Press, 1979.

Raz, Joseph. *The Morality of Freedom*. Oxford: Oxford University Press, 1986.

Rivers, Julian. *The Law of Organized Religions: Between Establishment and Secularism*. Oxford: Oxford University Press, 2010.

Roeder, Philip G. "Decentralization to Manage Identity Conflicts." In *Federalism and Decentralization in the Contemporary Middle East and North Africa*, edited by Asli Ümmühan Bali and Omar Dajani, 17–49. Cambridge: Cambridge University Press, 2022.

Rosen, Lawrence. "Islamic Conceptions of the Rule of Law." In *The Cambridge Companion to the Rule of Law*, edited by Jens Meierhenrich and Martin Loughlin, 86–100. Cambridge: Cambridge University Press, 2021.

Rowe, Paul S. "Neo-millet Systems and Transnational Religious Movements: The *Humayun* Decrees and Church Construction in Egypt." *Journal of Church and State* 49, no. 2 (2007): 329–50.

Saboori, Abdul Ghafoor. "Parwan Governor, Citing Supreme Leader, Says Previous Constitution Invalid." TOLO News, August 4, 2022. https://tolonews.com/afghanistan-179259.

Saeed, Abdullah. *Islam and Religious Freedom: A Sourcebook of Scriptural, Theological, and Legal Texts*, edited by Matthew Anderson and Karen Taliaferro. The Religious Freedom Project, December 5, 2014. https://berkleycenter.georgetown.edu/publications/islam-and-religious-freedom-a-sourcebook-of-scriptural-theological-and-legal-texts.

Saeed, Lutforahman. *Islam, Custom and Human Rights: A Legal and Empirical Study of Criminal Cases in Afghanistan after the 2004 Constitution*. Cham: Springer, 2022.

Salamey, Imad. "The Unmelting Lebanese National Pot." Canopy Forum, October 14, 2022. https://canopyforum.org/2022/10/14/the-unmelting-lebanese-national-pot/.

Sangiovanni, Andrea. *Humanity without Dignity: Moral Equality, Respect, and Human Rights*. Cambridge, MA: Harvard University Press, 2017.

Schaeffer, Katherine. "A Year Later, a Look Back at Public Opinion About the U.S. Military Exit from Afghanistan," Pew Research Center, August 17, 2022. https://www.pewresearch.org/short-reads/2022/08/17/a-year-later-a-look-back-at-public-opinion-about-the-u-s-military-exit-from-afghanistan/.

Scharffs, Brett G. "A Commitment to Religious Freedom as the Bond that Makes Us Free: Reinvigorating Security, Religious Autonomy, and the Good Society." *Review of Faith & International Affairs* 20, no. 4 (2022): 21–27.

Shklar, Judith N. "Political Theory and The Rule of Law." In *The Rule of Law: Ideal or Ideology*, edited by Allan C. Hutchinson and Patrick J. Monahan, 1–16. Toronto: Carswell, 1987.

Slye, Ronald C. "The Dayton Peace Agreement: Constitutionalism and Ethnicity." *Yale Journal of International Law* 21, no. 2 (1996): 459–73.

Stephens, Bret. "America's Crumbling Global Position." *New York Times*, October 26, 2021. https://www.nytimes.com/2021/10/26/opinion/us-military-russia-china-iran.html?searchResultPosition=2.

Stoeckl, Kristina. *The Russian Orthodox Church and Human Rights*. London: Routledge, 2014.

Stras, David R. "What My Grandparents' Experiences in the Holocaust Taught Me about the First Amendment." *New York University Journal of Law and Liberty* 15, no. 2 (2022): 476–89.

Tadros, Mariz. "Religious Equality and Freedom of Religion or Belief: International Development's Blindspot." *Review of Faith and International Affairs* 20, no. 2 (2022): 96–108.

Taher, Menna. "Tahrir Square: Where People Make History," *Ahram Online*, January 20, 2012. https://english.ahram.org.eg/NewsContent/1/114/32175/Egypt/-January-Revolution-continues/Tahrir-Square-Where-people-make-history.aspx.

Tahtāwi, Rifā'a Rāfi' al-. *An Account of a Stay in France by an Egyptian Cleric (1826–1831)*. Edited by Daniel L. Newman. London: Saqi Books, 2004.

Talbi, Mohammed. "Ibn Ḫaldūn et le sens de l'histoire," *Studia Islamica*, no. 26 (1967): 73–148.

Taylor, Charles. "Cross-Purposes: The Liberal-Communitarian Debate." In *Liberalism and the Moral Life*, edited by Nancy L. Rosenblum, 159–82. Cambridge, MA: Harvard University Press, 1991.

Thompson, Mark. "How Disbanding the Iraqi Army Fueled ISIS." *Time*, May 28, 2015. https://time.com/3900753/isis-iraq-syria-army-united-states-military/.

Tūnisī, Khayr al-Dīn. *The Surest Path: The Political Treatise of a Nineteenth-Century Muslim Statesman* [...]. Edited by L. Carl Brown. Cambridge, MA: Harvard University Press, 1967.

Tyan, Emile. *Institutions du Droit Public Musulman*. Beirut: CEDROMA, 1999.

United Nations. The General Framework Agreement for Peace in Bosnia and Herzegovina, December 14, 1995. https://peacemaker.un.org/bosniadaytonagreement95.

United Nations. Resolution 1378 (2001) / adopted by the Security Council at its 4415th meeting, on 14 November 2001. https://digitallibrary.un.org/record/452431?ln=en.

United Nations. Resolution 1383 (2001) / adopted by the Security Council at its 4434th meeting, on 6 December 2001. https://digitallibrary.un.org/record/454021?ln=en.

United Nations. Resolution 1386 (2001) / adopted by the Security Council at its 4443rd meeting, on 20 December 2001. https://digitallibrary.un.org/record/454998?ln=en.

Wacks, Raymond. *The Rule of Law under Fire?* Oxford: Hart, 2021.

Waldron, Jeremy. *One Another's Equals. The Basis of Human Equality*. Cambridge, MA: Belknap Press of Harvard University Press, 2017.

Walters, Mark D. *A. V. Dicey and the Common Law Constitutional Tradition: A Legal Turn of Mind*. Cambridge: Cambridge University Press, 2020.

Walzer, Michael. *Spheres of Justice: A Defense of Pluralism and Equality*. New York: Basic Books, 2010.

Weber, Max. *Economy and Society*. Vol. 2. Edited by Guenther Roth and Claus Wittich. Berkeley: University of California Press, 1968.

Weiler, J. H. H. "COVID, Europe, and the Self-Asphyxiation of Democracy." In *Democracy in Times of Pandemic*, edited by Miguel Maduro and Paul N. Kahn, 141–52. Cambridge: Cambridge University Press, 2020.

Weill, Rivka. "Acontextual Constitutionalism and the Relationship between the People, Constituent Power and the State: On Nicholas Barber's *The Principles of Constitutionalism*." *Jerusalem Review of Legal Studies* 24, no. 1 (2021): 94–112.

Wilber, Donald N. "Constitution of Afghanistan." *Middle East Journal* 19, no. 2 (1965): 215–29.

Woelk, Jens. "Opening Pandora's Box? On *Kovačević* and the European Court of Human Rights' Fundamental Criticism of the Electoral Ssystem in Bosnia and Herzegovina." *VerfassungsBlog*, September 1, 2023. https://verfassungsblog.de/opening-pandoras-box/.

Womack, Deanna Ferree. "Christian Communities in the Contemporary Middle East: An Introduction." *Exchange* 49, nos. 3–4 (2020): 189–213.

World Bank. "Metadata Glossary." DataBank. https://databank.worldbank.org/metadataglossary/worldwide-governance-indicators/series/RL.EST.

World Bank. "Worldwide Governance Indicators." DataBank. https://databank.worldbank.org/source/world-development-indicators.

World Justice Project. "2023 WJP Rule of Law Index." https://worldjusticeproject.org/rule-of-law-index/.

Yassari, Nadjma, and Mohammad Hamid Saboory. "Sharia and National Law in Afghanistan." In *Sharia Incorporated: A Comparative Overview of the Legal Systems of Twelve Muslim Countries in Past and Present*, edited by Jan Michiel Otto, 273–318. Leiden: Leiden University Press: 2010.

Zengarini, Lisa. "Cardinal Sako Warns Christians in Iraq Risk Disappearing." Vatican News, August 24, 2022. https://www.vaticannews.va/en/church/news/2022-08/cardinal-sako-warns-christians-in-iraq-risk-disappearing.html.

www.ingramcontent.com/pod-product-compliance
Lightning Source LLC
Chambersburg PA
CBHW031331230926
51848CB00001B/180
9789004533233